The *Woman* who *Prospers*

Principles that will transform
your family, finances and life.

MELVY DE LEON, NILDA PÉREZ
AND ANDRÉS PANASIUK

ISBN: 978-90-829791-6-9

Written by Melvy De Leon, Nilda Pérez and Andrés Panasiuk

Published by Compass – finances God's way

www.compass1.global

Scriptures are taken from the Good News Translation - Second
Edition © 1992 by American Bible Society.
Used by permission.

Design by Loulita Gill Design

The Woman Who Prospers

FOREWORD

One of the biggest problems that women have

I t is a scientifically provable fact that, when we talk about money, one of the biggest problems women have... is men! That is why, I wanted to write this book, I invited two insightful women, psychologist Melvy De Leon and entrepreneur Nilda Pérez to come alongside me and bring this book to life. I should admit that, despite having written so many other books, Nilda and Melvy really did not need my expertise to make this one happen.

The idea of writing "The Woman Who Prospers" was born in August 2005, during an event in Guatemala City, which we coordinated together with Mrs. Conny de Morales, a well-known Christian leader in her country of Guatemala and in the AGLOW organization. It was called "Women's Economic Summit" and was a resounding success. More than eleven hundred women from all over the country gathered in Guatemala's capital city to learn how to better manage what few or many resources they had available. I still remember how I felt when I got onto the stage in front of all those women - terrified! However, by the grace of God, the conference was warmly accepted...even copied, distributed, made into a PowerPoint presentation and packaged as a full-day seminar. The wide acceptance of the presentation led us to think that there might be many more women, from many continents, who could profoundly benefit from this material and that up until now only the women in Latin America had that possibility.

Since we launched the book in 2010 many tens of thousands of women have experienced our seminars and Bible Studies for women. Many thousands more purchased this book - making it one of our most successful.

This book was inspired by a poem written three thousand years ago by the mother of a king in the Middle East. This poem is in the 31st chapter of the book of Bible called Proverbs. It has been read over the ages by millions of women all over the world and talks about the characteristics of a "virtuous and exemplary woman." This victorious Proverbs 31 woman who, very much like you, faces the challenges of her times, models for us the principles, values, and practices that can make you successful in your family, your spiritual relationships as well as your financial life.

So, find a favourite reading corner in your house, grab a notebook, a pencil, prepare yourself a cup of tea or coffee and let's spend some time together exploring the journey to Whole-life Prosperity. We hope you will enjoy it. This book was written especially for you.

With much love in our hearts.

Dr. Andrés G. Panasiuk

INTRODUCTION

The Woman Who Prospers enjoys Whole-life Prosperity

A s a child, I remember looking forward to the arrival of summer so that I could participate in the camps that were organized by the Argentinian branch of Child Evangelistic Fellowship. One of the competitions they had for the kids was my all-time favourite - the potato race! The rule was that each participant had to place a potato on a spoon held between their teeth. To win, the player had to run a course and not only cross the finish line first, but also to maintain the potato balanced upon the spoon for the entire race! The concept of Whole-Life Prosperity, which we will use throughout this book, has a lot to do with this illustration.

In the race of life, it is not only important to successfully reach your financial, vocational, or economic goals, but also it is essential to reach these goals with the rest of our life intact. I am speaking of our time, talent, treasures (both tangible, like money, business, or home; as well as intangible, like love and respect from our children). We must avoid "dropping the potato."

Since 1990, I have been teaching, writing, and advising people from all social and economic strata's regarding this topic of Whole-Life Prosperity. After travelling over two million kilometres throughout Latin America and around the world, I have noticed that many people, especially men, act as if the road to economic prosperity is a 100-meter dash. They try to reach their goals is the shortest time possible. They risk time, talent, and treasures to obtain economic benefits that in the end do not lead to personal satisfaction.

The Woman Who Prospers enjoys an abundant life

As we begin our walk together throughout this book it is important to make clear from the beginning that the road to Whole-Life Prosperity is not an Olympic 100-meter dash. The best way to describe the road to Whole-Life Prosperity for you and your family is, in fact, a 20-km cross-country race… with hurdles!

Many believe that although money doesn't buy happiness, at least it helps. We say that because, in general most of us do not live in a rich society. We tend to think that if we did have the opportunity to live in a rich society, then we would be happy. This idea however, comes from the wrong premise and out of an erroneous paradigm, which is that material goods can satisfy our emotional and spiritual needs - like our need for happiness, love, or peace. This is the basic premise in a world philosophy that we usually call "Materialism".

The Lord Jesus clearly says, "Your true life is not made up of the things you own, no matter how rich you may be."[1] and this is a great truth. Easy to say, hard to understand. Think about this:

> Money can buy a house, but it cannot build a home;
> it can pay for an education, but it cannot purchase wisdom;

---

1   Luke 12:15

it can provide the resources for a heart transplant, but it cannot provide us with love.

Through the years I have noticed, contrary to public belief, that it is not poverty that rips families apart. From an economic perspective, the bad financial decisions and the accumulation of debts create tensions which become so great, that eventually they end up destroying the marriage relationship.

When we are poor, as my wife and I experienced this at different times in our life, the marriage relationship draws closer together. We work harder for the survival of the family. When one makes bad financial decisions in the home or when one spouse hides the money from the other, when debt piles up and we live out inaccurate money management principles, then resources begin to fail. The accusations of financial mismanagement begin to fly, then the insults come, the mistreatment and finally, separation and divorce.

Whole-Life Prosperity not only relates to our economic well-being, but also to the way we choose to live each day of our lives. It has more to do with an attitude of the heart and state of the soul rather than with the status of a bank account or a retirement plan.

An important idea to remember would be; the most important job in life is living. Where living means much more than merely existing. It means to stop running after material and superficial things and begin pursuing the more significant things in life.

PERSONAL SATISFACTION AND LEARNING TO LIVE.

Look at this short test to probe your knowledge on the subject of happiness.

In an interesting study published[2] by the American Public Broadcasting System about consumerism, it was discovered that

2   http://pbs.org/kcts/affluenza/diag/what.html

the percentage of Americans which said they had "very happy" lives reached its peak between the years 1957 and 2007. Choose the date you think Americans felt the happiest:

1) 1957   2) 1967   3)1977   4) 1987   5)2007

The correct answer is number 1. The amount of people that saw themselves as "very happy" reached its maximum peak in 1957 and has been pretty much stable or it has declined very little since then. It is interesting to note that Americans today consume twice as much as they did back in the 50's. Nevertheless, despite having less material goods, those Americans in the 50's felt as happy -or happier- than Americans today.

Learning to live means discovering the role or purpose for which we have been born. It means to put into practice the talents and gifts that life has given us, to focus on the transcendental things such as to serve and enrich the life of our partner, to love and teach our children, to develop our personal inner-lives, and to deepen our spiritual lives. Money comes only into play to help us on our way.

God wants you, as a Christian, to have life and life more abundantly.[3] However, the Lord Jesus himself tells us that, "True life is not made up of the things you own."[4] What does it mean then, to live life to the fullest?

Living our lives and living them to the fullest means to enjoying watching our children play in the backyard of our home. It means getting excited when we recite The Lord's Prayer for the first time with them next to their beds and giving them a good-night kiss. It means caring for other people's lives, helping to paint the house of the needy, fixing a single mom's car and listening to the broken heart of a friend until the small hours of the morning.

---

3   John, 10:10
4   Luke 12:15

Living our lives to the fullest means giving a helping hand to the poor, learning to restore the fallen and healing the wounded. It means to be able to look into our partner's eyes and telling him or her with all honesty "I love you". It means being able to become a servant-leader model for our children. It means leaving a mark beyond our own existence - a legacy for future generations.

This Biblical concept of happiness and personal satisfaction has little to do with the advertisements that we regularly watch on TV, or the current evangelist that teaches about materialism. If there is something I truly agree with, it is the concept that we mentioned earlier in this book - money doesn't bring happiness. Honestly, I don't really know how much it helps either.

Today you can begin walking on a different path. Today you can begin walking down a road that you have never taken before - the road to financial freedom, or as we call it in this book - the journey to Whole-Life Prosperity.

However, I cannot take you there. I can only show you the way. YOU are the only one that can decide to walk down this new path in your life. I cannot change the attitude you have towards life, the dynamics of your relationships nor the values in which you have anchored your economic life.

If you want to come out of where you are right now in your financial life, you will have to begin doing things differently – but you will have to do it yourself… and you must begin today. Are you ready?

WHAT IS WEALTH?

Not all that glitters is gold, and wealth is not everything that it seems to be. There is a very interesting book about this topic called

The Millionaire Next door[5] by Thomas J. Stanley and William D. Danko. At one point, it was one of the bestselling books in the USA and it is a window into the life of millionaires who live in the USA. Stanley and Danko dedicated years to this work and research to study the behaviour of millionaires in North America. I would like to share with you some very interesting things they discovered.

One of the discoveries that these authors made was that in the USA many people who live in expensive homes and drive luxury vehicles are not, in fact, very wealthy. The fact is that many people who have a great amount of wealth do not even live in the most sophisticated neighbourhoods.

Most people get confused when thinking about the concept of wealth. Wealth is different from income. Someone might have a very high salary but may not be rich. He or she may be spending every penny earned. Wealth, however is related to what we save and not to what we spend.

What is the secret concerning accumulating wealth, according to Stanley and Danko? It is rarely about having luck, receiving an inheritance, having a university degree, or even having a high IQ level. Wealth, in most cases, is related to a hardworking lifestyle, perseverance, planning and most of all to personal discipline.

What is the reason that proportionally, so few people are wealthy in the USA? Stanley and Danko say that most people, even making more than $10,000 dollars per month, are not wealthy because they tend to spend every penny they earn and even get into debt. These families believe that if they don't display their abundance then they are not successful. As you can see, the life of a millionaire in the USA is not as glamorous as it is portrayed on TV or the movies.

---

5   Thomas J. Stanley and William D. Danko. The Millionaire Next Door, the Surprising Secrets of America's Wealthy. New York; Pocket Books, 1996

The researchers of The Millionaire Next Door say that the three words that could properly describe the true wealthy people in the USA would be: frugality, frugality, frugality. It's not that they are stingy, but they hate wasteful spending. A husband may happily purchase a diamond ring for his wife's birthday, but that same husband would be upset if the bathroom light was left on the whole night long. One was an investment in love the other was wastefulness.

HOW TO BECOME A WOMAN WHO PROSPERS

Now that we understand what wealth really means and what goals we should pursue in search for Whole-life Prosperity and Abundant Life, we can devote the rest of the book to discover the secrets of reaching this unique kind of prosperity that we all long for.

Your Whole-life Prosperity is like a beautiful flower with five beautiful petals. Each one of those petals has warm and attractive colours and makes it an unusual and enchanting miracle. Without each element, it would not be such a stunning flower.

The same happens with your journey toward Whole-Life Prosperity. As with the flower, all the colours of a flower need to be present and to develop together for the miracle of beauty to occur. This book does not have steps, it has ingredients. Just like when you bake a cake - all the ingredients must be present to get the result you want.

If you acquire a lot of wealth, but you live your life your own way - just like a song Frank Sinatra used to sing - all your efforts will be in vain. If you have lots of money and financial success, but your children don't want to have a loving relationship with you, then you are not successful. If you have an excellent relationship with your children, but you cannot give them what they need because you mismanaged your resources then it is not an ideal situation neither.

Therefore, as you read this book, little by little, you should be able to work in each one of these five areas into your life.

Would you like to know the five areas in which you should become successful so you can be a Woman Who Prospers?

If you do, then join us in an exciting journey through time and space. We will travel to the Middle East, back in time to the 10th Century before Christ.

The secrets of a Woman Who Prospers are taken from the eternal legacy of a wise woman whose son became a king in the Northern part of the Arabian Peninsula.[6] We are only given her son's name. Her name was never recorded, but for the last three thousand years, tens of millions of women around the world have benefited from her wise advice.

Her words, like those of very few women in history, have been made eternal in the sacred writings of the Word of God. Today, we would like to invite you to study together the advice from the mother of King Lemuel. It is found in the Old Testament's Wisdom Literature in the 31st chapter in the book of Proverbs.

Welcome to the world of the Women Who Prosper!

Nilda, Melvy & Andrés

---

6   Proverbs 31:1, Good News Bible

The Woman Who Prospers

Teachings from the mother of King Lemuel
In the original text this poem is an acrostic,
each phrase begins with a letter of the Hebrew alphabet.
Good News Bible

PROVERBS 31:10-31

How hard it is to find a capable wife!
She is worth far more than jewels!

Her husband puts his confidence in her,
and he will never be poor.

As long as she lives, she does him good
and never harm.

She keeps herself busy making wool and linen cloth.

She brings home food from out-of-the-way places,
as merchant ships do.

She gets up before daylight to prepare food for her
family and to tell her servant women what to do.

She looks at land and buys it, and with money
she has earned she plants a vineyard.

She is a hard worker, strong and industrious.

She knows the value of everything she makes,
 and works late into the night.

She spins her own thread and weaves her own cloth.

She is generous to the poor and needy.

She doesn't worry when it snows,
because her family has warm clothing.

She makes bedspreads and
wears clothes of fine purple linen.

Her husband is well known,
 one of the leading citizens.

She makes clothes and belts,
and sells them to merchants.

She is strong and respected and
not afraid of the future.

She speaks with a gentle wisdom.

She is always busy and
looks after her family's needs.

Her children show their appreciation,
 and her husband praises her.

He says, "Many women are good wives,
 but you are the best of them all."

Charm is deceptive, and beauty disappears,
but a woman who honours the Lord should be praised.

Give her credit for all she does.
She deserves the respect of everyone.

Section One

The Woman Who Prospers learns to successfully manage her relationship with her husband and has clear priorities in her life

How hard it is to find a capable wife! She is worth far more than jewels! Her husband puts his confidence in her, and he will never be poor. As long as she lives, she does him good and never harm. She gets up before daylight to prepare food for her family and to tell her servant women what to do. Her husband is well known, one of the leading citizens. She is strong and respected and not afraid of the future. She speaks with a gentle wisdom. She is always busy and looks after her family's needs. Give her credit for all she does. She deserves the respect of everyone.

Proverbs 31:10-12, 15, 23, 25-27, 3

Chapter One

REALISES THE IMPORTANCE OF HAVING VALUES AND KNOWING YOURSELF

DR. ANDRÉS PANASIUK

"How hard it is to find a capable wife!
She is worth far more than jewels!
Her husband puts his confidence in her,
and he will never be poor".

Proverbs 31:10-11

If you want to be a prosperous woman, you should make sure you have the appropriate values and if you are married, your husband should embrace them as well. Proverbs 31:11 begins by saying that for things to run smoothly, your husband should be able to trust you. For this to happen, you both need to agree on certain crucial things in life.

1. God has made us different
2. God has given us different roles
3. God expects us to complement each other and not to compete

God has made us different

Not so long ago, a friend said to me, Look Andrés, single women complain that all the good men are already married, while the married women complain that their husbands are mediocre. This can only mean one thing: there are no men worth marrying!" As a man, I had a funny thought: With friends like these, who needs enemies!

The problem is not that there are no men worth marrying. The problem is that many times women enter into a marriage with one of two syndromes:

a. The Cinderella Syndrome: This is my Charming Prince and even though I am sure he must have some flaws, I cannot find any.

b. The Beauty and the Beast Syndrome: Yes. It's true. He is a beast, but give me four months and I will make a beauty out of him.

The truth is that there are things in our spouse that we would change immediately, things we will change throughout the years and things we will never be able to change.

God has created each one of us differently[7]. Each one of us have a very particular personality and usually opposites attract. How many times have we seen thrifty women marry men who don't know when to stop buying stuff? Or how many times have we seen men who are well organized in their finances marry women who are out of control with their spending habits?

I remember that my mentor, Larry Burkett, used to say, "If both are the same in a couple... then one is not needed." I have coached and counselled people since the early 1990's. Something that has helped me along the way is a format that I learned while I was a student at Trinity University in Deerfield, Illinois. I was once taught that most people can be grouped into one of four different categories: Dominant, Influential, Steady, and Compliant/Cautious.

---

7 Genesis 1:27

You might have read about these different types of personality profiles in the book by Tim LaHaye entitled, Spirit-Controlled Temperament. The author defines them as: Choleric, Sanguine, Melancholic, and Phlegmatic.

I would like to share with you a summary of each of these personality profiles and give you some key words that describe them. Then, I will attempt to show how each one of those personality profiles manages money and makes financial decisions. This is great section to read with your husband.

At the end of each explanation, I have also provided a couple of examples, one from the Bible and one from current history so you can see what types of peoples these profiles represent.

Dominant - Choleric Personality

People with a dominant personality have a natural tendency to control their work environment. They are usually firm, direct and strong-willed. They are typically aggressive and take risks. They obtain results through action. They work better in challenging environments.

Strengths	Weaknesses
Independent	Impatient
Seeks results	Thoughtless
Confident	Not detail-oriented
Direct	Bad listener
Good problem solver	Dislikes routines

The Dominant personality and her finances

In a finance environment, the Dominant personality makes financial decisions firmly, quickly, and impulsively. She has the passion to be successful. She is a leader in times of uncertainty and difficulty. However, it is hard for her to live on a budget and therefore she takes great financial risks and lives outside the limits of her financial capacity.

She tends to make current commitments solely based on future income. She does not adhere to the Principle of the Guaranteed Commitment - that is to say that she makes financial commitment without having a guaranteed way to pay for it. This type of behavior can lead her into serious debt problems, especially with loans and credit cards.

Her lack of attention to detail, her focus on goals and her stubbornness leads her, on many occasions, to develop financial problems in her business and in her relationship with her husband. She may sometimes place her family in financial risk to meet her business goals. She may also get in serious problems with the law if she is under strong financial pressure because in her mind the ends justify the means.

IN THE BIBLE	IN THE WORLD
Sarah, Abraham's wife Rahab, Rachel, Lydia, Zipporah	Hilary Clinton, Margaret Thatcher Cher (singer)

Influential - Sanguine Personality

People who have a sanguine personality have a natural tendency to relate to others. Generally, they are eloquent, friendly, extrovert and optimistic. They are also enthusiastic motivators that look for others to help them achieve their goals. They work better in a friendly environment.

Strengths	Weaknesses
Extroverted	Talk too much
Eloquent	Disorganized
Enthusiastic	Emotional

Optimistic   Problems with time management
Funny   Not detailed in nature

The Influential personality and her finances
In a financial environment, the Sanguine personality makes impulsive financial decisions often with her heart. It is very difficult for her to live within a budget and within her financial means. Because she is so positive about her future, she tends to make commitments and decisions based solely on future money - money that she has not yet received. She "presumes" on the future by not abiding to Proverbs 27:1 which warns against putting too much trust in future circumstances. She too, like the Dominant personality, tends to break the Principle of Guaranteed Commitment by entering a financial commitment without having the means to pay it.

This behaviour leads her to have serious problems with debt, especially loans and credit cards. She also develops financial problems in her business and in her relationship with her husband, especially if he has the Melancholic or Phlegmatic personality traits. She too can get into serious problems with the law if she finds herself under too much financial pressure.

IN THE BIBLE	IN THE WORLD
Mary Magdalene Rebakah, Abigail	Liza Minnelli, Oprah Winfrey Dolly Parton

Steady - Melancholic Personality

People who have the Steady personality have a high stability level and are naturally motivated to cooperate with others. They are patient, coherent and very reliable. They are friendly and forgiving. They are excellent team members. They work better in an environment that supports them and that is harmonious.

Strengths	Weaknesses
Peacemaker	Compromise values
Good listeners	Resist change
Patient	Avoid confrontation
Productive	Indifferent
Reliable	Very sensitive

The Steady personality and her finances

In a financial environment, the Steady personality makes financial decisions very carefully with anxiety and distress. When it comes to living within a budget and within her financial means she functions better than the Dominant or the Sanguine personalities. She is faithful at following rules and living with regulations. As soon as she learns how things are done, she is quick to do them right away. Once she learns the Biblical financial principles, she puts them into practice immediately. This helps her avoid getting into financial problems both in her family and in her business.

However, since she is so indecisive, careful, and hesitant regarding her future, she has a difficult time making decisions by herself. This hinders her from responding quickly to emergencies or taking advantage of rare financial opportunities. Additionally, her cautious nature, indecisiveness and lack of commitment stops her from climbing the corporate ladder.

This personality does not experience serious problems with debt, but due to her lack of initiative she will have problems surviving on her own especially if she loses her job. Financial tensions are exaggerated in a relationship when the Dominant personality marries a Steady personality.

IN THE BIBLE	IN THE WORLD
Dorcas, Martha, Anna Hannah	Michelle Obama, Nicole Kidman Mother Teresa

Compliant - Phlegmatic Personality

People who have the Compliant personality focus on doing things right. They are naturally detailed. They follow rules and regulations with ease. Typically, they seek quality and precision and have high expectations of themselves and others. They work better in a structured environment.

Strengths	Weaknesses
Analytical	Cold and distant
Organized	Unrealistic standards
Careful	Internalize feelings
Precise and detailed	Perfectionist
Compliant	Over analytical

The Compliant personality and her finances

In a financial environment, the Compliant personality is methodical and a perfectionist. She makes financial decisions very carefully, thoughtfully, and fearfully. Sometimes it seems to be almost impossible for her to make financial decisions. Her methodical and perfectionist character allows her to conform readily to a financial plan and wonders how other people cannot do it. She almost always lives within her means and is great at following rules and regulations. To tell the truth, she feels safer when functioning within the limits and boundaries.

Once she has established Biblical principles for her life, she never gets into serious financial problems for neither her family nor her business.

On the other hand, she finds it hard to break with tradition and be innovate with her finances. This characteristic stops her from responding quickly to emergencies or taking advantage of unique financial opportunities that come her way. She feels secure with businesses that do not pose a high level of risk. She invests in businesses that provide return on investments by growing slowly. In her business, money is earned methodically, little by little, over the years.

In the corporate world, she should avoid positions of leadership, such as being the president of an organization or corporation. If she finds herself in a leadership position, it would be wise for her to immediately designate a person to make all decisions concerning the business's management and operations. A key element that will help her to reach Whole-life Prosperity would be to fight against her instinctive distrust of other people's capacities to successfully fulfil a task.

Phlegmatic people rarely have serious problems with debt. However, they have serious problems with perfectionism, legalism, and the demands that they put on other people to perform. Their harshness and long memory of the sins committed against them keeps the Grace of God far away from their lives and heart and thus, Whole-Life Prosperity. Financial stress in the marriage relationship can occur due to weaknesses in her personality and the serious difficulties she has working in a team.

IN THE BIBLE	IN THE WORLD
Esther, Mary Ruth	Jackie Kennedy Onassis Jane Austen, Nikola Tesla

You can also visit www.compassglobal.eu/women to get more information about personality profiles. Knowing your own and your husband's personality profile will ease tension in the relationship and lower expectations. You will be successful in complimenting each other rather than competing in managing money.

God has given us different roles

When studying the Word of God regarding our marriage relationship, we see that we have some responsibilities that are optional, and some that are unavoidable.

To understand which ones are unavoidable and how to work with the optional, we will need to make certain paradigm changes. We will need to change the way we see and understand life around us.

It was Tomas Kuhn, who in his book, "The Structure of Scientific Revolution," made great effort to understand, apply, and spread the term paradigm throughout the world. Willis Harman from the Stanford Research Institute continued Kuhn's work and explained that a paradigm is "a way of perceiving, thinking, assessing, and making sense out of a particular vision of reality."

The Power of Paradigms

Paradigms are powerful phenomena in our lives. They are the lens through which we interpret the surrounding reality and provide the environment for decision making, both good and bad. Paradigms draw the map that allows us to understand where we are, where we want to go and how we will accomplish our goals.

Let´s suppose, for example, that somebody invites us to visit London. When we arrive, we rent a car, and we decide to go visit the person who invited us. Since we have never been in this wonderful city before, we consult a map. Across the top of the map it says, London. There are photos and description of the city on the sides of the map, but due to a printing error, the interior shows a map of New Delhi. We can have the best intentions in our hearts and make every effort to reach our destiny. We can have the best positive mental attitude in the world and even smile to everyone around us, but without the proper map, we are still completely lost!

Some years ago, Stephen Covey wrote a book called, "The Seven Habits of Highly Effective People." In it I found a story that perfectly illustrates how paradigms affect our attitudes and how powerful it can be to experience a paradigm shift. Covey tells about an incident that happened one Sunday morning while he was traveling on the metro in New York City.

> "People were quietly sitting on the train. Some were reading their newspapers, some were lost in their own thoughts and some were resting with their eyes closed. It was a scene of utter peace and quiet. Only the rickety noise of the train could be heard, and it marked it's route down the tracks.
>
> At the next stop a man and his children got on the train. In an instant, the whole environment changed. His children were loud and unruly. They ran from one side of the train to the other, throwing their toys to the floor. They began fighting among themselves and carelessly disrupting the other passengers. The father of the children sat next to me and immediately closed his eyes. He was disengaged and ignored the children.
>
> After a while, it was hard not to feel irritated. It was inconceivable that a father could be so insensitive as to let his kids run wild as he sat there disinterested. The other commuters were uncomfortable and irritated by the noise.
>
> Finally, with what I consider a great demonstration of patience and self-control, I turned around toward the father and said, "Sir, your children are disturbing many people. I was wondering if you could do something to control them a bit."
>
> The man slowly lifted his head as if regaining consciousness. It seemed that he was noticing the situation for the first time. He said in an almost whispered voice, "You are right,

I should do something. We've just come from the hospital. Their mother died a few hours ago. I am so confused... I don't know what to think. I imagine that they too don't know how to react to such a loss".

How would you have felt after hearing this confession from the lips of this man? You would have seen things from a totally different perspective, wouldn't you? And it would have made you react differently as well. Your irritation would have disappeared immediately. Your heart would have filled with hurt and compassion for the tragedy this man and his children were experiencing. You might have said, "Oh, I'm sorry! What can I do to help?" Everything would have changed in just an instant.

This is the power of a paradigm shift. It allows you to begin to see life in a completely different manner.

In this book, we will invite you to make some important paradigm shifts. They will challenge some ideas that have been embedded in your life from very early on. You need to reject the misleading, wrong maps and embrace the new ones to be able to become the prosperous woman that God wants you to be. Are you ready? Here are the new paradigms

God expects us to complement each other and not to compete

PROVISION COMES FROM ABOVE

The first paradigm change is related to the channel that God uses to provide for your family. "It is the Lord's blessing that makes you wealthy."[8] It is not our hard work, nor our intelligence, our education

---

8   Proverbs 10:22

nor our connections that make us rich. It is the blessing of the Lord. In this regard, the psalmist says, "If the Lord does not build the house, the work of the builders is useless; if the Lord does not protect the city, it does no good for the sentries to stand guard. It is useless to work so hard for a living, getting up early and going to bed late. For the Lord provides for those he loves, while they are asleep." [9]

It is not the hard work of the man or the woman which makes a family rich. It is the blessing of the Lord. He is our Yahweh Jireh. He is "The LORD, our Provider" and the owner of everything we have today and everything we will need in the future. King David says, "Everything in heaven and earth is yours, and you are king, supreme ruler over all. All riches and wealth come from you; you rule everything by your strength and power; and you are able to make anyone great and strong."[10]

Sometimes we act like the house is ours, the motorcycle is ours, the car is ours, and everything we own belongs to us. The truth is, the house does not belong to you, and neither does your business. Whatever you have, you have it by God's grace and it is by His grace that you even woke up today. It is by God's grace that you had the strength to go to work every day. He is the one who gives you the power to receive riches (be it much or little). Everything you have comes from the Lord.

I vividly remember the day in September of 1996 when our family doctor looked into my wife Rochelle's eyes and said to her, "The results of your tests say that you have skin cancer. This type of aggressive cancer runs in your family. It has already killed your aunt and your cousin. I see you have a six-year-old and a three-year-old child. If I were you, I would start making arrangements for their care because your future is truly uncertain."

---

9   Psalm 127:1-2
10   1 Chronicles 29:11b-12

That day, I took my daughters by the hand and suddenly understood how fragile life is. I thought about the important things that I needed to fight for and the senseless fights which I should never have started. That cool September day, I went to the small park in our town. I began to feel so powerless. I was an immigrant, 10,000 km away from my home town in Argentina. Away from those who would normally support and sustain me in crisis. Lonely and thoughtful, I understood clearly who was, in fact, my Provider; the Owner of my life and that of my Rochelle's. I understood then as I do now, the very fact that when I opened my eyes this morning and have the privilege of writing this book, it is only because of His grace and His love. God in his compassion provided, and my wife has been cancer free for over 25 years!

THE HUSBAND IS NEITHER THE PROVIDER OF THE HOME, NOR IS THE WIFE

The second paradigm shift we need to experience is in regard to the false idea that the husband is the provider and sole owner of the home. I know that this concept is deeply engrained in some cultures, but it is not Biblical. We should stop teaching it to our families and passing this idea on to the next generations. The LORD is our Provider. He sometimes provides through the husband, sometimes through the wife, sometimes through both and sometimes through neither!

I remember when we were newlyweds. Rochelle earned $400 per month in her job and I earned another $400 in mine. The problem we had was that the rent was $435. So, one salary did not cover the payment for the rent and we still needed money for transportation, food, clothing and utilities!

Nevertheless, the real crisis came just after we had been married for six months. Rochelle became seriously ill and had to stop working.

During the next six months, we experienced God´s hand as our only Provider.

I remember some mornings we would open our front door and find bags of groceries there. Somehow there was always just enough to get us through the week. Sometimes, at the end of a Sunday worship service an elderly lady came up to me and placed a little envelope in my pocket whispering, "Andres, this is God´s provision for you and Rochelle".

We must reject our prideful attitudes and the wrongful teachings from our ancestors and embrace the idea that everything we have is from God alone. All our finances, businesses, and material things, all that we possess comes for our loving Father.

One day of His grace is worth a thousand days of labour. You don't need to work harder and longer to succeed. You need God's grace.

Once we understand this basic principle, we can stop putting pressure on ourselves to provide for the home. We can stop humiliating the spouse that earns less than us and stop feeling inferior because we don't earn as much as the other. Husbands can stop feeling "less of a man" when wives earn more than them.

Developing this attitude towards one another in marriage is very important. When we do, each of us can become a team mate and a catalyst for the other person's prosperity and not a secret enemy. If God is blessing the fruit of your spouse's labour, rejoice with him... rejoice with her! Don't work against your spouse!

THE WIFE IS THE HUSBAND'S MAIN FINANCIAL ADVISOR

Another important paradigm we must destroy is the idea that wives are not knowledgeable or informed about the husband's business, therefore, they don't need to be consulted when husbands need to make important financial decisions. This is a huge mistake and a lie. Wives truly don't need to know all the details of their husband's businesses to be able to offer solid advice as to what should be done. She already knows the most important thing she needs to know: she knows her husband's character and she knows God. Our team at the Compass Global Alliance has been serving businessmen around the world for over 40 years and we have never seen a business go broke due to the wife's advice. Usually it is the husband's decision to go against his wife's advice that eventually leads it to bankruptcy.

I think that the reason we have so many women in our countries feeling discouraged and unfulfilled is because their husbands don't allow them to carry out the role that God has called them to play within their marriage. They feel frustrated! We could have many satisfied wives in our nations if husbands would allow them to be what God has designed them to be.

God tells us, "It is not good for the man to live alone. I will make a suitable companion to help him."[11] The woman has been designed to be a "suitable companion" or "suitable helper" for the husband. She is his main advisor in his life. Even though the wife may not understand the nature of her husband's business, she has a unique perspective on life. That perspective is extremely valuable when choosing a path for the husband's business.

Frits Phillips, former president of the Philips Company and son of its founder, once said, "He who does not ask for his wife's advice, misses out on half of God's wisdom." This is so true.

Therefore, one of the main roles the wife should have in the world of finances is that of an advisor. Each time men need to make a financial decision it is advantageous for them to listen to their wife's advice. She is their number one financial advisor. Men are

---

11   Genesis 2:18,

not obliged to do what she advises but are obliged to listen to and seriously consider what she says.

There is no one in this world that is more committed to the welfare and success of a husband than his wife. Making this paradigm shift together is essential for the prosperity of the family.

The same should happen when the wife needs to make a financial decision or develop some kind of business. "Victory is won through many advisors."[12]

THE MONEY IN YOUR POCKET IS NOT YOURS

Another paradigm shift we need to experience affects the way we manage money at home.

As I travel around the world, I notice that more and more women are joining the work force and starting their own businesses. Now I am starting to hear conversations like this:

"Darling, this is MY money and that is YOUR money. With MY money we can pay rent, housing expenses and entertainment. With YOUR money we can pay food, the children's education expenses … etc."

This way of managing money at home is extremely popular, but in my opinion, harmful. Managing money this way goes straight against God's design for the family. When God created Adam and Eve, He said they should leave their father and their mother to join their spouse and be only one flesh. Think about it: If you are only one flesh, how many financial plans should you have?

The way that many couples today manage money at home would be like my right arm not wanting to share the blood resources with

12   Proverbs 24:6

my left arm. Out of spite, my right arm makes a little hole in the vain and draws the blood out so that the left arm will not have access to it.

What do you think is going to happen to me? I am going to end up in the hospital… or in the cemetery? Our bodies were not designed to function this way. They were designed to share resources. That's the reason your mouth screams when you finger gets slammed in the door.

Now, the finger is very different from the mouth. They have different functions and don't look at all like each other. What do they have in common? Why is it that when the finger gets pinched the mouth screams? It is because they are both members of the same body. The same thing applies to our marriages. Husband and wives are one body. They should function that way.

A scientific study was carried out in Venezuela several years ago. According to an article published by Drs. Pareena Lawrence and Marakah Mancini, it was shown that in that South American country, only 45% of married couples make financial decisions together. I really think that these Venezuelan numbers are not very different from many countries around the world.

I would like to challenge you and your husband to start behaving differently:
1. Put all the money you make in the same pot.
2. Develop a Spending Plan together.
3. Assign each-other the management of different parts of the Plan.
4. Be faithful to your commitments and in your stewardship.

INSTEAD OF AN ALLOWANCE, A PORTION OF THE PLAN

Another problem I see in many countries on our continent, is the idea of a wife's allowance. This is the monthly or weekly amount of money which the husband arbitrarily gives to his spouse to cover the expenses of the home. This is not a portion of the Spending Plan that the wife manages. It is money that the husband gives to his wife with no relation to the family income or expenses. This is also an unhealthy tradition that we have received from the past and it needs to stop.

During my years of counselling I have become aware that most wives do not know how much money their husbands make or even what he spends. The only thing they know is how much money their husbands give them each week or each month. Lawrence and Mancini say that in Venezuela, for housewives who have no source of income, more than 88% of them receive this type of allowance.

We need to experience a paradigm shift and begin to function the way God has designed marriage: to be and act as one flesh. We should also develop and adjust together our Spending Plan and decide together who manages what part of that Plan. We, together, are one body and the secret for financial success in our couple is collaboration and not competition.

So, from now on, instead of saying "my money" or "your money" let's say "our money?" No! Didn't we admit that God was the Owner and Provider of everything? In fact, we say, "this is God's money and we are managing it". Let's become faithful managers of His money.

QUESTIONS AND PRACTICE FOR CHAPTER 1

We are all different because God has created us that way. He has also assigned us different roles. Based on these concepts, please answer:

1. Why do we have a difficult time agreeing in our marriage when we need to make financial decisions?

_____

_____

2. How can spouses help each other?

_____

_____

3. What agreements could you implement in your home to complement and collaborate with one-another?

_____

_____

4. Which marriage partner is best gifted to do the work of managing the finances of the home? Note: this refers to keeping accounts and making sure all payments are made on time.

_____

_____

Many people think that their riches come from their hard work. What does the Bible say?

Read these Bible verses and answer the questions based on God's wisdom.

5. What will bring riches to your life according to Proverbs 10:22?

_____

_____

6. Who is the true Provider of everything we have? Answer according to 1 Chronicles 29:11-12

_____

_____

7. Mention 2 reasons why the wife is the main financial advisor in the marriage.

_____

_____

Chapter Two

LIVES BY FUNDAMENTAL VALUES

DR. ANDRÉS PANASIUK

Five fundamental values that God expects us to abide by are:

The value of transparent communication
The value of order
The value of discernment
The value of perseverance
The value of self-control

1. *Honesty: The value of transparent communication*

The period starting at the end of the 20th century and the beginning of the 21st has been dubbed the communication era. The coming of the radio, television, records, satellite communications, CDs, DVDs and the launching of the Internet brought to the world a package of communication tools like there has never been before in history.

However, according to Nancy Terry, "today's couples talk about the important things in life only about 27 minutes per week[13], less than four minutes per day"! It is true that this study quoted by Terry was carried out in the USA, but I am under the impression that this may be true for many couples and that most couples regularly experience communication crises. That is why I want to highlight the importance of a clear communication. God is an excellent communicator. He determined that all creation should speak or communicate among themselves. My favorite 'communication Psalm' says, "The heavens proclaim the glory of God. The skies display his craftsmanship. Day after day they pour forth speech; night after night they reveal knowledge. They have no speech, they use no words; no sound is heard from them. Yet their voice goes out into all the earth, their words to the ends of the world."[14]

If all creation is talking with each other, why aren't we communicating here at home?

If you want to become a Woman Who Prospers, you need to find a way to communicate effectively and clearly with your husband. Tell him of your success and share your anxieties. Celebrate the victories and cry together about the losses.

Many years ago, I heard Dr. James Dobson, founder of Focus on the Family, talk about the difficulties that couples have in communicating effectively. He said that one reason for their problems was that women tend to have a more advanced vocabulary than their husbands. Women, in general, have a vocabulary of approximately 80,000 words, while their husbands only have around 40,000.

---

13   Terry, Nancy. Couples and Work: Staying Connected and Productive. Achieve Solutions. September 2007.

14   Psalm 19:1-4

I immediately thought - the problem that I have is that by the time I get home from work each day, I have already used my 40,000 words; and my wife, who spends the whole day with the kids, hasn't even started with her 80,000!

The truth is that science has finally discovered something that all the women have suspected for centuries: something is not right with the male brain!

In his book, How to Raise Boys,[15] Dr. Dobson explains that, between the sixth and seventh week of life, male babies experience a wave of the hormone called testosterone that, literally damages some areas in the brain. One of those areas is associated with speech and communication. Consequently, boys in general never reach the level of sophistication in the vocabulary as girls do and therefore have a hard time expressing their thoughts and ideas.

If you are married, read this poem together with your husband:

COMMUNICATION

Communication takes practice,
it's never perfect,
sometimes not patient,
sometimes not kind,
but you have to say
what's on your mind.

Lend an ear,
listen not just hear,
to the ones
you love so dear.

---

15   Dobson Dobson, James. Bringing Up Boys. Tyndale House Publishers, Carol Stream, Illinois.

Communication is not
a one-way street,
it takes two,
to conquer this feat.

Communication is hard you see,
but in the end, it is key,
to that great relationship,
we all want and need.

Open your heart,
say what's on your mind,
When you are partners for life
there's nothing to hide[16]

2. Order: The virtuous valour that should not be misplaced

Many times, people ask me, Andres, why should we write out or make a plan for managing our money?" For many of you, the answer to this question might be obvious, but since I come across it often, I am going to take a few lines to answer it.

We must be in control of the money and not allow the money to control us. There is no choice. If you want to become a Woman Who Prospers, it is critical that you have a plan or a method to manage your money. Both in business and at home, you must control money and not let money control you.

If you were born and raised, like me, in a country with high inflation rates, then planning the way you spend the money is a matter of life and death. The difference between eating and starving at the end of the month is related to the way we have shopped during the previous weeks. You become a mini Minister of Economy.

Having a plan brings order. As human beings, we were created with a natural tendency to move away from chaos. The universe has an order; the solar system has an order; the human body has an order which is so impressive that we still have trouble understanding how such complexity can function so harmoniously. God is a God of order.[17]

Society tends to establish order. That is the reason laws exist. Each time we lost the social order (or the financial one) in my country, we were willing to do anything to bring it back, even if that means giving up some of our democratic liberty.

You will notice that after a natural disaster like a typhoon or a tornado, people will immediately start cleaning up and making efforts to restore and bring back order.

Everything has an order. The universe seeks balance. We all need some type of coherence in our life. Human beings have an inner tendency, placed there by their own Creator, to seek order in the mist of disorder.

That is one reason you purchased this book. It is because you know that there are areas in your financial life that need to be put back in order. When they are restored to order then you and your family will be blessed and benefit from it.

Multi-millionaire King Solomon advises us to "Be aware of the condition or state of your sheep and cattle, because wealth is not permanent."[18] In his days, of course, you could not go online and monitor your bank account. There weren't any financial statements.

---

17   1 Corinthians 14: 33 and 40
18   Proverbs 27:23-24

45

There were cattle and sheep. There wasn't a "stock exchange" to invest in; you invested in your livestock and their offspring. To apply this proverb to our day and age, we could say, "Be familiar with developments in your bank account and investments. Pay attention to them. Have a clear idea of how much money you have and how much you owe; because wealth does not last forever."

Throughout this process towards Whole Life Prosperity, we must have a plan for managing money. We must know how much income is coming in and how much expenses are being paid out. We must have a clear idea of what is flowing through our hands. To fully develop our plan, we should analyze how we are spending the money right now. We should then think through the kinds of adjustments we need to make to rearrange expenses so that our spending is efficient and less than our income.

This plan is a simple tool that any person with basic education can carry out. However, at the same time, it is a powerful tool to successfully reach the end of the month and reach our financial goals. Developing a simple plan to manage the money will ensure the proper steps are being taken towards bringing back order and eventually peace in to our financial lives. Visit our web site for more information on developing a spending plan.

3. Discernment: The value that clarifies needs from wants

Before explaining the two concepts of needs and wants, I would like to point out that it is not bad or sinful to have wants or desires. God gave us desires. He wants to be the one to fulfil them. To be able to reach the prosperity you long for, it is very important that you are able to distinguish between needs and desires. A good rule to remember is: satisfy the needs first then satisfy the desires if there are financial resources available to do so.

Needs

In my psychology classes in the university I studied the famous Maslow hierarchy. This hierarchy divided human needs into five general areas that graduated up from the most basic one, physiological, to the highest one, the need for self-fulfillment[19]

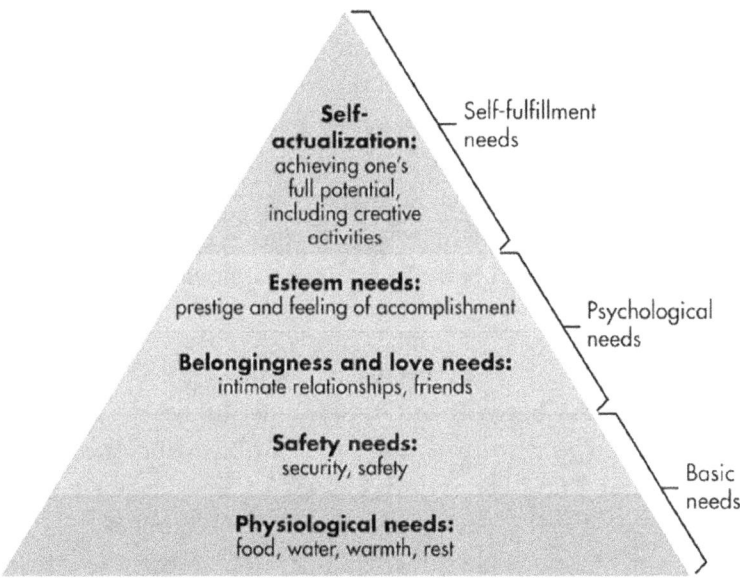

For the purposes of our study, I will use the term needs to define Basic Needs from the chart above. From a financial perspective, this pertains to all the material things that we need for survival: food

---

19   McLeod, Saul. *"Maslow's Hierarchy of Needs"*. *Simply Psychology. N.p.,*
      16 Sept. 2016. Web. 29 Aug.2017.
      http://www.businessballs.com/maslow.htm

and water, warmth/clothing, safety/security/housing. This could also include: transportation and health care. Hence, we must place our needs at the highest priority level. We should seek to fulfill them first. That is where the financial resources should go without any doubt or delay.

Wants

As we analyze the purchases that we need to make, we realize that not everything we buy is a need, as defined above. Whatever does not fit into the need category is considered a want. We can define wants in two sub categories: higher quality or desire. An example of higher quality is when you go shopping for food and you choose a higher quality piece of meat rather than the one that is on sale. You have satisfied a need with something that has a higher quality. On the other hand, a desire is simply something that you don't have and would really like to have, even though it does not fit into the above definition of a need. An example would be a new dress or a new pair of shoes.

Higher quality could be explained as wanting a good piece of steak instead of a hamburger. Food is a basic need for the body, but in this case, you want to satisfy this need with a product that is more expensive and of a better quality: a steak. This applies to all the other areas of real needs in your life. You could buy a dress in a thrift store or you could buy it couture. In both cases, clothes are a need, but the way you satisfy the need can quickly transform the purchase into a want.

Desire could be explained as buying a new TV and sound system, a new table for your patio, another set of earrings or buying another property. You should satisfy your desires only after having satisfied your needs and if you have the financial resources to do so.

Therefore, before going shopping it is very important to be clear about what is a need and what is a want. Nowadays people have the tendency to say, "I need a computer" or "we need a camera" when what they really should be saying is "I'd love to buy a new computer" or "we would like to have a camera."

Unfortunately, in the last thirty years we have gone through a conditioning process that has made us exchange our wants for our needs. This only creates an anxiety that impulses us to satisfy that "need". We have been deceived and now believe that having new clothes to start a new job is a need when in reality it is a want. The clothes you have right now still may fit and do the job that they need to do ... So, we end up spending our money on things that we don't really need and take the money from the things we really need (whether immediately or long term).

In some circumstances, it is better to purchase things of better quality. Things that will last a lifetime rather than things of a lower quality which will need to be replaced every certain amount of years. On the other hand. Also, keep in mind that just because something is on sale does not mean that it is a good investment. If you purchase ten packs of detergent because it is on sale and then run out of money to buy milk or basic needs for the family then you have made a bad investment. This is a typical case in which it is not a good idea to "save by spending".

When the grocery store is offering a 'buy one get one free' sale on milk then I would immediately take advantage of the offer (especially if I have kids at home). Milk is an element of daily consumption and a basic need for my survival. Laundry detergent can be replaced with cheaper options.

The other concern with purchasing products in large quantities, just because they are on sale, means that you will have your cash tied up in this product as it sits on the shelf. This is an issue that many business owners face daily. Believe it or not, managing the finances of a home is very much related to the way you handle things in a business, even the economy of a country.

4. Perseverance: The value of persistence and patience

"But the Spirit produces love, joy, peace, patience..."
Galatians 5:22

The fourth value that we can agree on are the values of persistence and patience. Let's analyze the following Bible passages together.

In the Bible, James exhorts us to develop patience. He says in his universal letter, "My brethren, count it all joy when you fall into diverse temptations; knowing this, that the trying of your faith works patience."[20] The word patience can be defined as perseverance or consistency.

Another Bible version translates this passage as follows, "Consider it pure joy, my brothers and sisters, whenever you face trials of many kinds, because you know that the testing of your faith produces perseverance. Let perseverance finish its work so that you may be mature and complete, not lacking anything."[21]

The type of patience that I am talking about is defined as being steadfast, continuing to be righteous during difficulties, trusting in God and waiting on Him. It is an active patience, standing strong and holding the line. What patience is not is - surrendering to our own desires and removing ourselves from difficult circumstances, becoming depressed, and numbing our pain with food, shopping or alcohol.

---

20   James 1:2-3 (KJV)
21   James 1:2-4 (NIV)

Exercising patience from the financial point of view requires that we get out of our prevailing attitudes and cultures. It requires that we start looking at life as a 25 km race. It means that we learn to be constant through time and not surrender to circumstances. After a fall we get up, wipe the dust off our clothes, and keep moving forward.

Our financial race is not a 100-meter dash. We cannot view it as a short-term commitment. Only those who see their finances as a long-distance race will be the ones who eventually achieve a higher level of prosperity. Confucius said, "Our biggest glory is not that we have never failed, but that every time we have fallen, we have got back up again."

5. *Self control: The value of good behavior*

"But the Spirit produces love, joy, peace, patience, kindness, goodness, faithfulness, humility, and self-control…"
Galatians 5:22-23

The fifth and final value that I would like to emphasize for attaining Whole-life prosperity is the value of self-control. One could define it as the ability to perform something that we have been asked to do, to modify a behaviour, to postpone an action and to behave in a socially acceptable manner without being guided or directed by another person.

Self-control is a vital element and clear mark of mature character in an individual. Without it, it is impossible to make a financial plan and carry it out. Without self-control, it is impossible to put into practice the secrets and ideas that I will provide for you in the next few pages.

Defeat in this area of our lives, is what keeps financial aid counselors busy year-round. People today spend an average of one dollar and ten cents for every one dollar that they earn. Lack of self-control is causing an unprecedented amount of bankruptcies, both personal and business.

To understand the seriousness of the lack of self-control, we only need to cast our eyes over to the huge weight-loss industry or the serious health issues that are plaguing us today.

Take a look at this small excerpt from a song of desperation, written by singer/artist Ricky Martin called, *What Day is Today?*[22]

> What day is today? I cannot take it….
> …without control of my actions, bad mood,
> I get up.
> There is no sun, no summer, my garden
> has dried up,
> there are no more flowers and my love
> has left…

I am not surprised his love left. I would have left too! It is very difficult to live in peace and communion with a person who does not have control over his or her actions. His reaction to adversity has allowed his "garden of interpersonal relationships" to dry up.

An old Chinese saying explains it like this:

> He who knows himself has insight.
> He who conquers men has power;
> He who conquers himself is truly strong.
> He who knows when he has enough is rich.[23]

---

22   https://genius.com/Laura-branigan-self-control-lyrics
23   Tao Te Ching 33 Book of Wisdom, fundamental in the philosophy of Taoism and Chinese religion.

Self-control is a vital building block in the construction of Whole-Life Prosperity. It is the manifestation of your spiritual maturity and a fruit of the work of the Holy Spirit of God in your life. Learning to value self-control with your finances is key.

Finding a New Pathway

If you continue to believe the lies of those who want to get rich at your expense, then you will never advance with your finances. There are a series of phrases that we have come to believe, but eventually they all ruin our chances of succeeding financially:

- Treat yourself. You deserve it!
- What is one more spot on a tiger?
- Buy and save
- Buy now, pay later
- This is a once-in-a-lifetime offer
- The devil pays the last bill
- You need one of these…
- Live it up!
- Why wait?

"Plant a thought and you will reap an action", is a well-known saying based on the words of the English novelist Charles Reade, "Plant an action and you will reap a habit; plant a habit and you will reap character; plant character and you will reap a destiny!"

The capacity to reach your financial destiny is in your hands: you should have the burning desire and absolute personal commitment to perservere with your plans.

Some years ago, Alicia, a friend of the family, had a stroke. The blood clot eventually lodged itself in her brain. This caused a stroke and half of her body became paralyzed. The lack of oxygen had destroyed vital cells used for the flow of information in her brain.

She was affected in her speech and physical mobility. Several years later she had experienced a full recovery. You would have never imagined that she had been paralyzed and mute for almost a year and a half.

What happened? How was she healed? Her body began to do something amazing. A blood clot was in her brain. Her system started forming and growing new communication pathways of nerves and vessels around the blood clot! Alicia's brain began to recover the lost functions.

Even though this is not the experience of all patients with this type of condition we can learn a valuable lesson. Even the body has a natural tendency to fight for order and life. Our body will continue with perseverance to keep working until the time that total chaos causes it to perish.

We are not meant to surrender to 'destiny' or 'fate.' We are meant to conquer the land and subdue it. We are designed to be victorious.

One of the most precious gifts we have received in life is our will to decide. Some time ago, while reading Stephen R. Covey's "The 7 Habits of Highly Effective People", I encountered the story of this well-known Jewish psychiatrist. I'd like to share it with you.

Viktor Frankl was a determinist psychiatrist. He believed that things that happened to you during your childhood determined what you would become as an adult. Once the personality parameters were established there wasn't much one could do after that to change them.

Frankl eventually became a prisoner of the Nazis and was taken with his family to a concentration camp. Almost all his relatives died in the camp and even Frankl was a victim of countless tortures and horrible pressures. There were days when he thought he would not see a new tomorrow. One day, alone, tired and naked, he found himself in the corner of the tiny room where they kept him captive.

Searching through his thoughts he discovered what he later called "the last of man's freedoms" (a freedom that nobody could take away from him).

Frankl noticed that the Nazis had the power to control his surroundings, the environment in which he moved and lived, but they did not have the power to control how he would react to his situation. He realized that he still possessed one freedom - the freedom to choose his own attitude. He could decide if he would let the circumstances destroy him emotionally or if in the midst of them, he would continue to grow as a person. He kept his inner spirit warm during the harsh winter rule of Nazism in his country. During the horrors of the Nazi concentration camp he discovered a fundamental principle of human nature - between the stimulus and the response, humans have the freedom to choose and the power to decide their own attitudes.[24]

God has given you the freedom to choose. How are you going to react to the circumstances you are in today? You can choose to be desperate and bitter. You can choose to give up or can choose that today, will be the last day that money dominates you.

Despite facing a difficult financial winter, you can choose to grow your inner spirit. You can choose today, to recognize which areas of your personality are not working and decide to seek a new route in order to reach your goals. You can do it. You were made to conquer the land, not to be swept away by your circumstances.

Let's walk together toward prosperity.

---

24   Stephen R. Covey, The 7 Habits of Highly Effective People. Pages 69 and 70.

QUESTIONS AND PRACTICE FOR CHAPTER 2

If you are worn out and weary of your circumstances, read this poem together with your husband.

I love you
I love you, because you are
my love, my accomplice, my all,
and when we walk arm in arm,
we are much more than just two.
Your hands are my caress,
my daily reminders.
I love you because your hands
work hard for justice.
I love you, because you are
my love, my accomplice, my all,
and when we walk arm in arm,
we are much more than just two
Your eyes are my lucky charm,
against the bad days,
I love you for your beauty
that waters and seeds the future
... love is not a halo
or a naïve idea
and because we are a pair
we are never alone
I love you, because you are
my love, my accomplice, my all,
and when we walk arm in arm,
we are much more than just two.

-*Mario Benedetti.* Portions and adaptation of the original poem[25]

---

25   http://www.paularcher.net/translations/mario_benedetti/te_quiero.html

What a great truth! There is tremendous synergy of power between a well-rooted couple. "When we walk arm in arm we are much more than just two". This is one of the biggest secrets of a Woman Who Prospers: arm in arm with her husband, they are much more than just two!

To practice. Get used to differentiating among needs, desires of quality (DQ) and desires (D). Write next to each word the letters N, DQ or D accordingly. Compare your answer with ours in the following page. Let's get to work! (If you are married, do it together with your husband)

N = basic need of the human being
DQ = Desire of quality: basic need satisfied with a higher quality solution
D = Desires. They are not basic needs.

1.food		17. Sweets	
2. Pants		18. Perfume	
3. Shoes		19. Video	
4. Steak		20. Soda	
5.ice cream		21. Birthday party	
6. Vacations		22. Eating out	
7. Television		23. Tourism in the mountains	
8. Radio		24. Tools	
9. Computer		25. Telephone	
10. Coffee		26. Toys	
11. Education		27. Dress	
12. House		28. Cleaning rags	
13. Housing		29. Special gifts	
14. Transportation		30. Pets (dog, cat, etc)	
15. Car		29. Special gifts	
16. Potato peeler		30. Pets (dog, cat, etc)	

Answers:
N = basic need of the human being
DQ = Desire of quality: basic need satisfied with a higher quality solution
D = Desires. They are not basic needs.

1.food	N	16. Potato peeler	D
2. Pants	N	17. Sweets	D
3. Shoes	N	18. Perfume	D
4. Steak	DQ	19. Video	D
5.ice cream	D	20. Soda	DQ
6. Vacations	N	21. Birthday party	DQ
7. Television	D	22. Eating out	DQ
8. Radio	DQ	23. Tourism in the mountains	DQ
9. Computer	D/DQ	24. Tools	DQ
10. Coffee	D	25. Telephone	DQ
11. Education	N	26. Toys	D
12. House	DQ	27. Dress	N
13. Housing	N	28. Cleaning rags	DQ
14. Transportation	N	29. Special gifts	DQ
15. Car	DQ	30. Pets (dog, cat, etc)	D

Explanation of some answers:

Item 8: Radio: radio has a different role from the one the TV has. Radio is an important source of information, socialization and community contact. That is the reason that we have placed it as DQ. In some of the rural towns it could become an "N". TV is, mostly, an entertainment item.

Item 9: Computer: it depends on what you use it for, a computer can have very important roles at home (organization of finances, kids' education, internet research, etc.). In other cases, it is used solely as an entertainment item.

Items 12 and 13: House/Housing: if yet housing is a basic need for the individual, the house is not. One could satisfy the housing need by renting an apartment for example, instead of buying one.

Item 20: Soda (water or juice with gas): as with the other carbonated drinks or juices, it is a DQ because drinking liquids is a basic need of human beings. The juices and sodas are a more expensive choice to satisfy that need.

Items 22 and 23: Eating out and tourism: recreation is a need, but we can do it without the need of eating out or having to do tourism. These are "quality" choices to satisfy the basic need.

Item 29: Special gifts: to love and feel loved is a basic need for the human being. However, we could show our love toward others without necessarily having to buy them something. It is a choice to satisfy the need with a much higher quality.

Chapter Three

HAS A GENUINE CONCERN FOR FOLLOWING BIBLICAL PRIORITIES

DR. MELVY DE LEON

One day after returning from our honeymoon, I woke up in the middle of the night and looked at the man I loved there, next to me, peacefully sleeping. While I looked at him, I thought, How long will he be by my side?" But then, I realized, "He is now my husband ... he belongs to me!" That sense of belonging that women have is what gives us security.

In his book "Love Must Be Tough"[26] Dr. James Dobson mentions that the ingredient of "respect" is absolutely fundamental to all human relationships, especially in marriage.

The way we behave every day depends largely on how we respect or disrespect the people around us. The way spouses relate to one another depends on mutual respect and admiration. That is one of the main reasons whey disagreement between spouses almost always originates from a lack of respect somewhere in the relationship.

---

26   Dobson, James. Love Must Be Tough. Kingsway Publications, 2001

When a woman respects her husband, the anticipated result is that she "brings him well every day of her life." This type of woman is a blessing and not a problem for her husband. The good comes to him and she is the source of that blessing. She supports and encourages him, and he is faithful because she helps him "every day of his life". When a wife behaves like this, her husband trusts her completely, he believes in her! Her care in the administration of the home enhances the wealth of the family, and she does not lack anything regarding household things.[27]

The Woman Who Prospers looks to provide wellness for her husband, takes care of her children, takes care of her possessions and her good name. She does it, because she knows well the priorities in her life.

The woman is…
And God made them,
to be man's companion,
to his own image, with excitement,
from a man's rib,
to be his partner.…
to be his blessing.
All women are the same,
gifted with a high level of wisdom,
with autonomy of thought… authentic,
with a sixth sense that makes the difference.
They have incomparable beauty, some physically,
others intellectually, but in both cases, unending perfection,
that surround us in their dreams, sweetly.
They are laser-focused,
on defending their loved ones even with her own life,
in their eyes, these women have the light of day,

---

27   Expository Commentary: The Bible Knowledge Commentary (Old Testament). Book 4. Editors John F. Walvoord and Roy B. Zuck

62

they have the power to raise a warrior from the depths of defeated.
They are mothers, friends, they are lovers,
created with the magical tenderness of love,
they are the support of triumphant gentlemen
they live in a beautiful world… they are simply the best.

Sergio Rodríguez

This poem declares a powerful truth: A woman has the power to raise an already defeated warrior.

Proverbs 31 not only speaks of "The Woman Who Prospers," but also about the family that prospers because of her. The Woman Who Prospers has not only prospered herself. Her prosperity spills over to the rest of her life as well. She prospers in her family, in her relationship with her husband, in her relationship with her children, and in her spiritual, academic and economic life.

Her secret is not only running to win the race God placed before her but also doing so without sacrificing other important matters in life, like children, family, spouse and relationships.

Many women in developed countries today, when they reach the age of 40 or 50, and are at the top of the "ladder of success," realize the ladder is leaning against the wrong wall! They turn around, they look at their husband and say, "I've seen you somewhere… you look familiar to me…" Of course! Because they have shared a house but never built a home. They lived under the same roof, but they were never a "couple." These women have a high-end social status but have missed the opportunity to truly enjoy their joy of having a family.

The practice of whole-life prosperity reminds me of a time when my husband and I had been married for eight years and he lost his job. I worked in a well-known organization and had a very well-paid job. It was enough to cover the family budget; however, as a good Latin American woman, I had grown up with the idea that the man is the 'provider' of the family. So I talked to my husband about it almost every day and demanded he would find a job. This harassment continued until one day Dr. Andrés Panasiuk came to our country to participate in an important event and I took the opportunity to share my frustration with him.

My husband had no job and to me, it was his responsibility as a man to bring sustenance to the home. However, I immediately got the answer I least expected when Andrés asked me, "How are the bills paid at your home?" I answered, "With my money."

It was obvious that he had been able to identify the problem that I still was not able to see. Then with great diplomacy but firmness he reminded me that God is the Owner of everything and the sole Provider of the house.

You know very well that women are very sensitive. Our self-esteem is quickly affected, and we cry when we feel misunderstood, so you can imagine how I felt when Andrés continued speaking. He tenderly said, Melvy, God is your Provider. Jahweh Jireh is the provider of your family. You should feel blessed that today He provides through you. Tomorrow He will provide through your husband, and sometimes He will provide through neither of you. God is predictable because you know He always provides, but He is also unpredictable when it comes to the way He does it. Go home, talk to your husband and ask for his forgiveness."

You cannot imagine the change that my husband and I began to experience after that day. Today we live with 40% less income, my husband faithfully serves the Lord full-time and we walk the beautiful adventure of waiting for God's provision every day of our lives… and experience God's faithfulness month after month after month!

You can also experience God's provision and faithfulness in your life. You will be able to reach the end of your life and, then, say with the Apostle Paul, "I have fought the good fight, I have finished the race, I have kept the faith."[28]

Together we can say to the Lord, "Here are my children, here is my husband, we love each other, and we go to church together. I am willing to receive the crown of righteousness that You has set aside for me in Heaven." The author of the Book of Proverbs said, "Find a wife and you find a good thing; it shows that the Lord is good to you."[29] I long to experience a victory like this virtuous woman described in Proverbs 31 achieved.

The husband who has found such a good team-member has God's goodness. When he finds out that it is the wisdom of this woman which builds her house,[30] and that her spirit of sacrifice makes that building experience possible, then, according to the Word of God, she has earned her family's praise. "Her children show their appreciation, and her husband praises her."[31]

Life priorities

God is in control of our lives and our future. We must simply align our priorities so that we act according to His divine will. Then He will bless us. Unfortunately, this world pushes us to have our family priorities upside down and this pressure is shown in so many ways.

In our Biblical counselling sessions my husband and I can clearly see that Christians have problems with setting our priorities in a proper, Biblical order.

We all have priorities in life. However, God gives us four or five priorities in His Word that are fixed, and we must place them at the

---

28   2 Timothy 4:7 NIV
29   Proverbs 18 :22
30   Proverbs 14:1
31   Proverbs 31:28

top of all other priorities in our lives. May I share them with you?
Here they are:

1. *God*

"Jesus said: Love the Lord your God with all your heart,
with all your soul, and with all your mind".
Matthew 22:37

Our relationship with God must be at the top of the list. He must
be our priority number one in both of our lives. If you are a believer,
you know Christ has purchased you with His blood. Your number
one priority in life should be God. Not the church of God. Not
the work of God. Not the Word of God. God. Sometimes we
get confused and think that if we go to church often, then we are
putting God as priority in our lives. The BIble teaches that if we
want to develop a personal relationship with Him, we should spend
time talking and communicating with Him. Unfortunately, instead
of using things to serve God, many people use God to get things.

Many have the idea that God is a supermarket where you go ask
for things, God give me this; please give me that." "Heal me; love
me; fix this problem for me." We end up having an unhealthy
relationship with God - a relationship where we are the centre, and
not God. Aladdin rubbed the lamp and the genie would come out
and say, "I'll grant you three wishes." We treat God as that genie.
We are living in a consumer society and have learned to 'consume'
God. We treat Him as if He were a 'service provider.'

I have two daughters and maybe you have children as well. Can you
imagine that every time your child came to see you and talk to you,
he would say, Forgive me, Mommy. Lend me the keys to the car,
mommy. Give me money, mommy. Buy me shoes; I need new pants,
Mommy." One day you're going to wonder, "Doesn't my child have
any other way of relating to me besides asking me for things?"

Sometimes as parents it seems that all our children ever do is ask us for money or things and we become like their slaves who give them everything they ask for, right? But that is not the kind of relationship we want to have with our children. We long for communication and personal connection. In the same way, God wants to have a personal relationship with us - a personal connection. The Lord wants to have a healthy relationship with His sons and daughters. He is not a force or a mind in the universe that is lost out there. No! He has a personality and wants to relate to us on a personal level. He likes to develop personal relationships in the same way that a parent would like to develop a personal relationship with a son or a daughter.

Many times the people in our churches believe in God as an "entity." They relate to God the same way they relate to the government. Our country's government exists, in the same way, they believe that God exists. The government of our country acts, and they believe that He acts. The government actions affect your life, God's actions affect our lives...

But the question is: Can you have a personal relationship with the government? Of course not! The government is an entity, it doesn't have a personality. Christians often relate to God in the same way. The issue is not going to church, attending more services, giving more in the offering or singing in the choir. All this has to do with our service to God, but nothing to do with our relationship with Him. The Lord wants us to relate to Him in a personal way and put that relationship first in our lives.

2. *Our spouse*

*"Submit yourselves to one another because of your reverence
for Christ. Wives, submit yourselves to your husbands as to the
Lord. For a husband has authority over his wife just as Christ
has authority over the church; and Christ is himself the Savior*

of the church, his body. And so wives must submit themselves completely to their husbands just as the church submits itself to Christ. Husbands, love your wives just as Christ loved the church and gave his life for it. But I want you to understand that Christ is supreme over every man, the husband is supreme over his wife, and God is supreme over Christ."[32]

The second place in our life must be occupied by our spouse. He is the most important person that God has given us to accompany us along the path of our life. Your spouse should be your priority number two, immediately below your relationship with God. Many times as women we place our children as a priority over our spouse. However, it is very important to remember that we cannot be good mothers if we are not good wives first. It is necessary to have first a well-founded relationship with our spouse so we can provide our children the affection, understanding and education they need. There can be no well-founded family if Mom and Dad don't have a firm relationship.

This is the reason your spouse should come immediately after God. You have to spend time with him. You have to develop a friendship, because in a few years, your children will get married; they will start a family of their own and you will be alone with the spouse God gave you for another 20, 30 or 40 years. Today there are people who live to be 100 years-old ... What is going to be the type of relationship you will both have as a couple as you age? If you don't develop a firm relationship now, it will be much harder later on.

In order for your husband to take second place in your priorities, it is important that you fulfil the command to submit to him. This is a subject that many women in today's society do not like. I did not like it either, but it was due to ignorance and a misunderstanding of the true meaning of "submission."

---

32   Ephesians 5:21-25 and 1 Corinthians 11:3

To submit to the husband is not a blind act of slavery without knowing in which direction you are walking. Submission, as the Bible teaches, seeks to please, anticipates the need of the other, and supplies it. In the same way Christ submitted to the Father, so you must recognize that the husband is the head, the leader, the guide, the person responsible for your marriage. You are both one and the same body. The wife depends on the husband to protect her from danger and is subject to 'everything' as is fitting in the Lord. He also supports her, holds her in high esteem, and values her above everything else in this world.[33]

According to Ephesians 5:21, the husband also submits to his wife. He loves her with a divine love (In Greek, Agape) and always seeks her welfare. He gives himself for her, he denies himself and his desires in order to please her. He sanctifies her, he sets her apart only for him and there is no other woman in his life. He purifies her and maintains the purity of the relationship as established by the Word of God.

By practicing these Biblical instructions and the truths of Scripture, he sets her apart. She is made glorious, beautiful, and lovely. He praises her; he compliments her and sees no flaw, stain or wrinkle in her. He loves her as he loves himself because they are one body. He sustains her, appreciates her and gives her great value, treating her with respect. He cares for her, covers her with his tender love, his affection, security and protection. He leaves his parents to become one only with her.

Andrés, who is constantly traveling through Latin America, says he thought some of the safety instructions people give on the airplanes were wrong. He would read this information on the safety card and disagree with it, "In case of emergency, put your oxygen mask on

---

33   1 Peter 3: 1-2

first and then place it on your child." He thought, "That's wrong. How come these people tell me I should put my oxygen mask first? I should put the mask first on my child, and then I should put it on myself."

He was troubled by these instructions until an airplane steward explained it to him. The flight attendant said to him, "You have to wear the mask first, because the child cannot fend for himself. You have to be conscious first. If you faint in the middle of an emergency, who will take care of that child? You and the child could suffer. But if you remain strong, it doesn't matter that the child gets weak for a moment, because you can take care of her." The same thing happens in the family. Mom and Dad need to have a firm relationship before they can take good care of their children. If the parents do not have a well-founded marriage relationship, they will not have the philosophical and spiritual bases set for the children to grow emotionally healthy as well. That is, unfortunately, what we see many times in families who get divorced and are destroyed. It takes two people to run a family.

Here is a key concept for men: men need to understand that his wife is his 'number one financial advisor.' God gave the woman the task of being 'a suitable help.' That is why we find so many frustrated women with 'lemon-sour faces' up and down our country. That's because the husband does not let her fulfil the mission that God has given her on earth.

3. *Children*

*"Parents, do not treat your children in
such a way as to make them angry.
Instead, raise them with Christian discipline
and instruction."*
Ephesians 6:4

Our children should be one of our top priorities in our lives. Even before work, and any other activity. They should come immediately after our spouse. The Scripture is clear about this.

We must give our children what cannot be bought with money -our being, our history, our experiences, our time. Let's make sure we share our lives with our children, because no psychological technique will work if love does not work.

Unfortunately, family foundations are cracked because of a lack of values, wise decisions and poor relationships between spouses. The lack of good role models has severe effects on the relationship between parents and children. Many families give the appearance that everything is OK and, out of shame, do not seek advice over time. Many couples are not talking to one another and are on the brink of divorce. Others experience violence inside the family unit.

In my work as a therapist, I provide counsel to many families. It is very common for the mom to come asking for help for their children. They say, "Look, here is my son. Please help me. I don't know what to do with him. At school I was told I should take him to a psychologist." I usually respond that I will gladly help, but first I need to have a meeting with the father and the mother of the child. Then the objection arises, "But... why? It's the child who needs help!" My standard response is, "I'm sorry but it's a requirement to talk to you and your spouse first."

When I talk to the husband and wife together it is very common to see that the couple's relationship is not very healthy. They are the first to need urgent help. The question is: How can they help the child, if they are not well? If they don't have a healthy relationship? If they don't agree on how to raise and educate him? After a couple of sessions, then we can talk to the child. Three weeks later, they come to tell me that the child is changing. Many times, their selfishness is so strong that they cannot bring themselves to admit that it was them who took the first step toward change. I believe that if the head is well, the body is also well.

Those mothers who have learned to truly serve their families have established clear priorities for their lives and have learned to set aside the consumerism and materialism that surround us all. Those mothers have learned to give themselves first to the children and not to give them merely toys and games. They give their children time, attention and communication. We must give our children priority in our agendas, even when we are full of important activities.

Some people -even in ministry - do not agree with me, but I have set a rule in my life that after working hours, I try not to take calls that would divert the attention that I owe to my daughters. I think that at work or in ministry there always can be somebody who can replace me. Nevertheless, at home I know that as a mother I have the privilege of knowing that no one can replace me -nor should I allow that to happen.

4. Our work or ministry

Proverbs 31 provides us with a beautiful picture of a working woman who lives a balanced life and emphasizes her home. The wife's job is not so much at home but for the home. The Bible does not say that a woman should be confined to the four walls of the house, but rather that she is involved in things related to the home.

There are many reasons why women have been involved in all kinds of jobs. Married wives work for several reasons. Some work to bring additional income to the family. Others, to develop their creativity. Even others because they enjoy getting out of the house and being in a work environment. Some of us who have flourished as professionals and have jobs outside the home, carry a heavy load of at least seventy to eighty hours a week of work - including our employment and household chores. Husbands should take note and help with this burden so that the wife can keep a healthy, balanced life for her family.

Widows, divorced women, single mothers and those below the poverty line often have to work for the basic needs of their families. For them there is no choice. But for married couples, working outside the home is a decision that must be made in full agreement with the husband and in prayer so that both support each other and fulfil the priorities that God has established for the well-being of their family.

Many women today have become a "workaholic" (addicted to work) and their motivation is to make as much money as they can. I do not say that it is wrong for us to flourish as professionals, business women or entrepreneurs. I am one myself. My recommendation to you would be not to spend all the energy you have at your workplace, so you can have energy to fulfil the privilege God has given us as wives and mothers. We should not allow work to rob us of the quality time we owe to our family. Let's not forget that at work anyone can replace us, but no one can replace us at home. God will ask us to give an account for how we have managed that which He has entrusted to us.

The same work principle can be applied to us who work in ministry. We cannot allow the ministry to push our family into the background of our lives. I encourage you, my dear friend, to keep your balance in life. God has given us the ability to multi-task. We are mothers, wives, friends, professionals, servants of the Lord … all at the same time!

In addition to all other commitments, we are committed to sustaining our own family and fulfilling the ministry that God has entrusted to us.

The apostle Paul, says, "But if any do not take care of their relatives, especially the members of their own family, they have denied the faith

and are worse than an unbeliever."[34]
He also expresses, "Be sure to finish the task you were given in the Lord's service."[35]

To his assistant Timothy, being trained to loom after the growing church he wrote, "A church leader must be without fault; he must have only one wife, be sober, self-controlled, and orderly; he must welcome strangers in his home; he must be able to teach; he must not be a drunkard or a violent man, but gentle and peaceful; he must not love money; he must be able to manage his own family well and make his children obey him with all respect. For if a man does not know how to manage his own family, how can he take care of the church of God?"[36]

5. Everything else

The main credential for a ministry or a valid job is an organized and well-cared family. In the past, putting ministry or work before the family has created many problems for the people of God. That attitude has created family tensions and has brought many headaches to Christian parents, missionaries and Church leaders.

Finally, after those four are in place, we can choose other goals we would like to accomplish in life. After God, spouse, children, work and/or ministry, you can put anything else you want - the rest of your extended family (parents, in-laws, cousins), education, vacations, financial goals and so on…

Now, I encourage you once again to think about how you spend your time during the week and compare them with the Biblical priorities for our lives. If you look closely, you will find out that

---

34   1 Timothy 5:8
35   Colossians 4:17
36   1 Timothy 3:2-5

the order of godly priorities is diametrically opposed to the way the world pushes us to spend our time each week.

A generation of rebellious children to the gospel, bitter wives and grieving parents are the result of not having maintained our godly priorities. That is why it is essential that each week you plan together with your family to spend a day together - a real, full day! If you need to leave home and neighbourhood to do it, go ahead! Spend a day every week with your own family. It is not important where you will go together. It's not important if you spend money or not. The most important thing is that you all will be together - at least, once a week!

The Woman Who Prospers influences the whole family with her character

Let's begin by establishing that children inherit not only physical but also combinations of temperament, personality, and character traits from their parents. However, in the premarital counselling that we developed at church, we have observed that couples are unaware of this obvious reality. So many young people come to marriage with the idea that when they wed, they will change the way their spouse dresses, eats, walks, and -especially- that they will transform the spouse's character. The wife says to her husband, "I want you to stop visiting your family and relate only to mine so you can learn from them and be like me!" If you think this way, you're in for a big surprise. You are not building a healthy relationship with your husband.

If you want to help your husband develop a character that pleases Christ, you must change yourself first! You also need to work on your character. "In the same way your light must shine before people, so that they will see the good things you do and praise your

Father in heaven."[37] This is the only 'light' that will cause a reaction in others, including your spouse.

The place to change the behaviour of a man is on the inside and not on the outside. It is very important that as women, we understand this principle to be useful instruments in the hands of God to help our husbands in the development and strengthening of a character that looks more and more like Christ.

Two of my favourite passages in the Bible say, "I do not judge as people judge. They look at the outward appearance, but I look at the heart,"[38] and "Be careful how you think; your life is shaped by your thoughts."[39]

It is true that each human being inherits certain peculiarities that make up his character. Nevertheless, when we become "daughters of God" we inherit the character of Christ, and this is the light that shines through us.

How many of us have not justified our bad temperament by saying that we inherited it from such-and-such parent or grandparent? Tim La Haye in his book *"Temperament Handbook"*[40] says that temperament is the combination of certain characteristics with which we are born. "Character" is our civilized temperament, and personality is the "face" we show others. Character shows who you really are. It is the result of your natural temperament modified by instruction, education, basic attitudes, beliefs, principles and motivations received during childhood. Character is also called as the "soul" of a man, and is made up of the mind, emotions and will.

Let me also give you an example on what should not be done with the character of a husband.

---

37   Matthew 5:16
38   1 Samuel 16:7
39   Proverbs 4:23
40   La Haye, Tim. Temperament Manual: Discover your potential.

A young couple began their married life with practically nothing. Then the wife realized her young husband did not have a stable job, they didn't have a decent home to live in, he hadn't completed his studies, he went out to work all day and they never prospered. This continued until one day, she put him between a rock and a hard place. She told him that she wanted a house in a specific neighbourhood. She also wanted him to buy her a washing machine, a dryer, and gave him her wish list. If not, everything was over.

The young husband was in love with his wife, so he went searching for a better job as a salesman. He had not even received his first salary when he rented a beautiful house in a rising neighbourhood. Then, with a credit card, he bought the most beautiful washing machine, dryer and furniture she had ever seen in her life.

The wife organized a party and invited her friends to show them all the beautiful things they had in such a short amount of time. She looked happy and enjoyed showing 'everything' she had. But soon they realized the sad truth: the husband's monthly salary was not enough to pay for all the luxuries she wanted. So they had to move back to live in the humble place where they started.

How many homes have been destroyed and couples divorced because couples do not work on their character. They don't work on their spiritual lives and fight for things that are not really worth fighting for.

You will also need to be aware of your role as a woman and ask yourself, "Am I a woman who is submissive and obedient to the teachings of the Bible?" It is only after asking yourself this difficult question that you will be ready to support your husband. In order to do this, we will analyse together the characteristics that distinguish men from women.

Men want to be providers. The centre of their lives is not the home - it is his work, the factory or his profession. He is a conqueror. He is aggressive. He goes in search of the daily bread and has a target he want to shoot at. He is cold, calculating, logical, and impersonal. He looks at the basics. He is not detail-oriented. He is a natural born-leader. He wants to have the responsibility of the house and he likes to project himself into the future. He feels a sense of discouragement because he has it tough, all day long. He must earn the daily bread by the sweat of his brow ...

On the other hand, they are negligent. They need to be reminded of things because they forget their commitments. Many men do not want to take responsibility for the home. It is the job of a woman to remind him of his role.

In Latin America, we have many strong men and few true men. The strong men come home and yell, want everything for themselves, they want to be served and they behave like if they were the centre of the Universe. Nevertheless, when they need to be responsible, fix things, take care of the children's -or wives- emotional needs they are weak. They look and sound strong, but they are actually weak.

Women - we are insistent, like a constant drip -and this creates a danger to the relationship. We have feelings of loneliness. We are possessive. When we are depressed, we go and buy something. When we fight with our husband, we go and buy something. When we are happy, we go and buy something to celebrate!

Understanding how each one of us 'works' helps us all relate to each other a little better. A husband can bear any scorn, any problem, any abuse, as long as this does not come from his wife. There is nothing that discourages a man's life more than his wife's lack of trust and understanding.

God has given women the gift to be sensitive. He has given her the capacity to encourage others to rise up in the face of adversity. Those qualities help us to provide encouragement to our discouraged husband's heart.

In the Scriptures, God set apart a full chapter to discuss the multifaceted role of the daily tasks that the woman performs from the time she rises until dusk. "How hard it is to find a capable wife!"[41] This statement reaffirms the joy a man has in his heart when he finds such a woman.

Women can also be wise or foolish. A wise woman will help build up her husband's character. She will encourage him to be honest and develop trustworthy relationships, at work and at home. She will encourage him to build a healthy relationship with God. She will challenge him to be wise in the management of his time and the resources God has given to him.

In this book we will learn the remarkable qualities of the Woman Who Prospers. Those are: hard work, wise investments, good use of time, planning ahead, caring for others, respect for her spouse, the ability to share with others in need, live out Biblical values with her neighbours, acquire wise counsel and practice the pious fear of the Lord.

---

41   Proverbs 31:10

QUESTIONS AND PRACTICAL APPLICATIONS FOR CHAPTER 3

1. Why should God be the number one priority in your life?

2. What do you think are the problems we can see in families where mom and dad don't have a well-grounded marriage?

3. What do you need to do in order to make your marriage stronger? Talk to your husband about it. Work with him on implementing these ideas

4. Which of the following causes can negatively affect the relation you have with your children?
   - Inadequate relationship with husband
   - Lack of responsibility on your maternal role
   - Lack of time with the children
   - Another cause

5. How can you change them?

6. What ministry are you carrying out for the Lord? How much time do you spend on it? How is your family involved in it?

Exercise: Write which are the five most important Biblical priorities you should have in your life. If your spouse is reading this book with you, then you each need to make your own notes… and don't copy from each-other!

Priorities (in order of importance)

1.
2.
3.
4.
5.

Now I would like to encourage you to write down how you are spending your time during the week. Count the amount of hours you spend sleeping, at work, if you go to church once or twice a week and spend 4 to 10 hours there, if you go to a club several times a week or attend a women's meeting, if you have a second job, if it takes you more than two hours to come back from work, (that would be about 14 hours per week that you spend travelling), if you take time on the weekends to go camping or sightseeing… Write, in broad categories, how are you spending your time, how many hours are you dedicating to each one.

For example:

Activity	Amount of hours per week
Sleeping (8 hours for 7 days)	56 hours
Working (8 hours for 5 days)	40 hours
Eating (4 hours for 7 days)	28 hours
Commuting (2 hours for 6 days)	12 hours
Watching TV (2 hours for 6 days)	12 hours
Church (various activities)	8 hours

Now it's your turn. With all honesty, write down the way you are spending your time:

Activity   Number of hours per week

_____   _____

_____   _____

_____   _____

_____   _____

_____   _____

_____   _____

_____   _____

_____   _____

Now, look closely at the two lists. Observe the Biblical priorities and compare them with the categories and number of hours you spend each week in each activity. Do you see a problem? What do you see?

If you have a spouse, share the results, and develop a plan together in order to live a more balanced life.

Section Two

The Woman Who Prospers learned to successfully develop her personal skills

A capable wife [...] keeps herself busy making wool and linen cloth. She brings home food from out-of-the-way places, as merchant ships do. She gets up before daylight to prepare food for her family and to tell her servant women what to do. She looks at land and buys it, and with money she has earned, she plants a vineyard. She is a hard worker, strong and industrious. She knows the value of everything she makes and works late into the night. She spins her own thread and weaves her own cloth. She doesn't worry when it snows because her family has warm clothing. She makes bedspreads and wears clothes of fine purple linen. She makes clothes and belts and sells them to merchants.

Proverbs 31:10, 13-19, 21-22, 24

Chapter Four

UNDERSTANDS THE IMPORTANCE OF HER PERSONAL DEVELOPMENT

DR. NILDA PÉREZ

Today's World and Your Prosperity

The Woman Who Prospers:

- Is a woman with exceptional character and unbreakable principles.
- Develops her character.
- Is of uncompromising virtue.
- Is governed by the highest values.
- Earns the respect of all those around her.
- Tries to fulfil the will of God.
- Is admired and respected by people to the point of exalting her.
- People know what is trustworthy in her life and she does it.
- Is someone with whom everyone wants to be around because she builds into their lives.
- Always keeps her word.
- Creates unfaltering loyalty and security.
- Always tells the truth.

The postmodern world in which we are living is characterized by the uncertainty and constant changes that threaten our economic stability. God wants us to be women of principle with firm values such as honesty and integrity. Where there is honesty and integrity, there is prosperity. We are seeing a moral decadence in the world in which we live.

Today, more than ever, the world needs the active contribution of the "virtuous woman." More and more we see how women have the desire to contribute to their family finances. For this reason, if we want to give economic strength to our family, we must be women that constantly develop the skills that God has given us. God created each of us with specific abilities and gifts. It is our responsibility to develop them to the fullest. As we develop those skills, God will give us greater abilities. As the beloved apostle of Jesus says, "Beloved, I pray that you may prosper in all things and be in health, just as your soul prospers."[42]

Now notice that John not only wrote "I pray that you may prosper," but "I pray that you may prosper as your soul prospers." He linked economic prosperity with the prosperity of our emotions, our will, and our state of mind. God's plan is for us to grow in our finances as well as in our spiritual lives. The woman who is described in Proverbs 31 was a woman who knew how to first grow spiritually and then develop her skills to be effective in the various roles she has.

God is interested in our being and not just our doing. He knows that it is dangerous to put great wealth into the hands of someone who is not spiritually mature enough to handle it. You can see dramatic evidence of this in the lives of people who have acquired economic wealth through the system of this world and then become full of bitterness and stress, neglecting and destroying their families.

---

42   3 John 2

God's plan is for us to enjoy "Whole-life Prosperity" in our lives. He does not want us to live in poverty. He has given us creative minds and abilities to develop our lives to the full. All of us were created to experience the prosperity and abundance that God has for us, "according to His riches in glory."[43] When we are living according to His complete will in our life, there is purpose and direction, and we are filled with the true joy "that surpasses all understanding."[44] God wants people to prosper. What happens many times is that we do not have the financial wisdom to apply the principles that are established in the Word of God.

Why do some people fail to prosper in their Christian and personal lives? First, they have a distorted theological appreciation. They consider that having wealth is bad and sinful. There are Christians who live under the influence of the theology of poverty which maintains that in order to be spiritual, it is necessary to get rid of all wealth and material goods. The greater the poverty, sacrifice and suffering, the greater the spiritual growth. This is a theological distortion of the gospel.

Many women live under the oppression of the enemy who do not let their lives flourish to their maximum expression of what God wants. This oppression leads us to have a spirit of dependence, of poverty, of limitation and disbelief, and lack of hope.

The statistics show the decline in the lives of many women. According to the World Bank, there are approximately 1.3 billion poor people around the world of which 70% are women. According to the National Institute for Research on Women, poverty in women is directly related to their lack of autonomy and economic opportunities, difficulty in accessing financial resources, education and services, and participation in the decision-making processes.

---

43   Philippians chapter 4 verse 7.
44   Philippians chapter 4 verse 19

In contrast to this, it is wonderful to see how more than three thousand years ago the Bible describes a woman that flourished to her full potential. Today, we think that the 20th century was the promoter of women's liberation, yet God had already left it exemplified in His Word thousands of years ago. Let's open our minds and hearts to break away the oppressive bonds that have limited the progress of women. I invite you to cut that generational tie today. We have to yearn to want more. God has wonderful things for your life – Do not limit yourself – put yourself in the hands of the Lord and let Him perform miracles in your life.

The good news that we have as Christians is that Christ died on the cross to give us life and an abundant life. There are many women that live without ever experiencing that abundant life that Christ promised us. This does not mean that life in Christ is all rosy, or that we never have any problems. It means that despite being in the middle of the storm or in adversity, Christ will provide the courage and strength for us to persevere and continue on. God gave these encouraging words, "I alone know the plans I have for you, plans to bring you prosperity and not disaster, plans to bring about the future you hope for".[45]

On the other hand, the theology of stewardship determines that we are responsible for that which God has entrusted us. But, in order to comply with that responsibility, you must first discover what God has given you. He has gifted you with intelligence and understanding for you to use to the benefit of the Lord.

I would like to address the importance of developing ourselves and releasing the potential God has placed in us. The Larousse dictionary defines the word development as "extending, unfolding what is wrapped up, enlarged, expanded." It also defines the word potential as "something that is possible, that can happen or

45   Jeremiah 29:11

come into being." God has called us to develop and to release the potential that He has placed in us. Do not limit yourself; you can achieve all that He has destined for your life. Learn to improve your performance, discover and expand your talents, and build a well-being environment. Maybe you've tried once and failed, but God is a God of opportunities.

Let me tell you a story which, when I first heard, struck a chord in my heart:

There once was a farmer who had many animals, and one day a good friend came to visit. The farmer, wanting to show off his farm, took him out on a walk. When they reached the henhouse, the friend said, "Look Carlos, that there is not a chicken, it's an eagle." Carlos answered, "No! It's a chicken. Look! It eats like a chicken, walks like a chicken, and looks like a chicken."

The friend answered, "I'll prove to you that it's an eagle and not a chicken. I'll climb that tree, and I'll make it fly, and when it does, you'll see it is an eagle." The friend climbed the tree, and made it fly. The bird suddenly sees all the chickens pecking corn on the ground, identifies with them, and ends up landing next to the chickens.

"I told you! It will never fly because it is a chicken," said the farmer. But the friend answered, "What happened is that I released it too low and too close to the henhouse, and when it looked at the chickens, it identified with them. Look, I'll climb up to the rooftop and you'll see it fly away." The friend again climbed up, grabbed the bird and released it into the air. This second time, the bird rose higher but again landed to peck corn with its chicken friends.

"It's useless to keep trying," said the farmer to his friend, "it will never fly away because it is a chicken." However, for a third time, the friend decided to go to a hill far away from the henhouse and then release it. By now, the sun was at its peak, and eagles tend to fly guided by the sun. When Carlos' friend got in a position to release the bird, the bird caught the sunlight, soared and gained height.

"I told you it was not a chicken!" he shouted to his friend. "When it didn't see the henhouse or the chickens, it focused on what it really was and soared into the sky like a true eagle!"

Each one of us is an eagle that God has created to soar high in life, but many times, because we are living in a henhouse, we conform to pecking corn with the chickens. We have wings with which we are able to fly high, but we do not use them. It is time to leave the henhouse we live in and begin behaving as God destined us to be.

A Personal Development Plan

Our nature, as daughters of God, is to live in a continuous process of development and learning. In order to develop our personal skills, we must each establish a personal development plan. Personal development is not about being different from or 'better' than other people; it's about being more of who God wants us to be. That means we don't compete with other women, but rather with ourselves. We must challenge ourselves to grow to the highest expression of the woman that God has truly created in us. Our task is to learn to listen to the voice of God and thus discover what purpose He has for our lives.

We must come to life with a passion and a daily desire to grow and contribute. God calls us to leave the henhouse and begin behaving like eagles.

ENOUGH PASSIVITY, START WORKING ON YOUR LIFE!

It is imperative that you know where you are going in life and actively endeavour to accomplish your goals. You need to set clear objectives and firm expectations and make dreams that will become true. Woman, dare to dream!

Through my years of coaching, I have seen that one of the most important limitations women have in order to succeed is their own attitude. Our attitude in life is related to our faith. To please God, we must have an attitude of wanting to do things and trust in Him for results.

Jesus, our Lord, says, "Have faith in God. I assure you that whoever tells this hill to get up and throw itself in the sea and does not doubt in his heart, but believes that what he says will happen, it will be done for him. For this reason I tell you: When you pray and ask for something, believe that you have received it, and you will be given whatever you ask for."[46]

Let's have faith in God. Let's dream about the future God has placed in our heart, let's work with all our being, and let's trust God fully for the results. The Lord teaches us that if we trust in Him, He will do it. Many times, we do not throw ourselves into the business calling we have, because we compare God's resources with our own.

Let me share with you my personal testimony and how God modelled my heart by teaching me to rely on Him.

After seven years of experience working in the consulting industry, there came a time when I felt frustrated, deflated, stuck and unhappy with myself. I wanted to do so many things; however, I thought that I did not have the abilities to do them. In a given moment, I realized that I had low self-esteem and that I was full of fears and doubts that were limiting the plans God had for my life.

During a mission trip, God was glorified in an extraordinary way and gave me this word that forever changed my life. There

---

46   Mark 11:22-24

are moments in which you recognize that God is speaking to you because there are things in your heart that nobody else knows. So, when He uses someone who doesn't even know you to talk to you specifically about what is in your heart, it's because He wants to teach you something. You might relate to that and know how special it feels to go through such an experience.

God spoke to me specifically about fear, a fear that was limiting me. During that time, I did not fully understand the whole message He wanted me to get. But after returning from that mission trip, when I went back to work, I found out that I had been fired. My first reaction, very human, was complaining to God why these things happened to me if I had been doing His will and working for Him. But, little by little, God began to mould my heart and during the next four months, He began to teach me to fully depend on Him. You know, when we learn to depend on the Lord, we see miracles in our life. Even when we foresee hard circumstances ahead, God will never leave us!

Then, one morning when I was praying to the Lord, those words that the Lord had given me through a pastor came to my mind, "You have been limiting yourself." These words became a challenge for me to get up and claim the promises God had for my life. I decided to believe the word of God and began developing some proposals for professional services in the consulting business. Suddenly, I started to notice something different about me. I felt more secure, more decisive, very cheerful, and wanting to be successful. I realized that God had transformed my heart, and my attitude had changed. When my heart was transformed, and my attitude changed, I began to see miracle after miracle. Doors began to open, and the insecurities began to vanish.

The key is to let God transform our attitudes. We must constantly be aware of our attitudes because they determine our behaviour. Out of this, our lifestyle, openness, and habits are born. Our behaviour influences our relationships with others. If our attitude is negative, it will affect trust, collaboration, and our willingness to share with others. If our relationships are affected, we will have problems in achieving our results. The level of achievement or scope of achievement will be limited. If our results are negative or unexpected, they will affect our attitude and repeat the negative cycle again and again.

In figure 1 we can see a cycle showing how attitudes impact results. We can define attitude as an inner feeling that is reflected and has an impact in behaviour. Our attitude, as discovered by Viktor Frankl, is a predisposition to respond in a certain way with favourable or unfavourable reactions to something that has happened to us in life.

FIGURE 1[47]

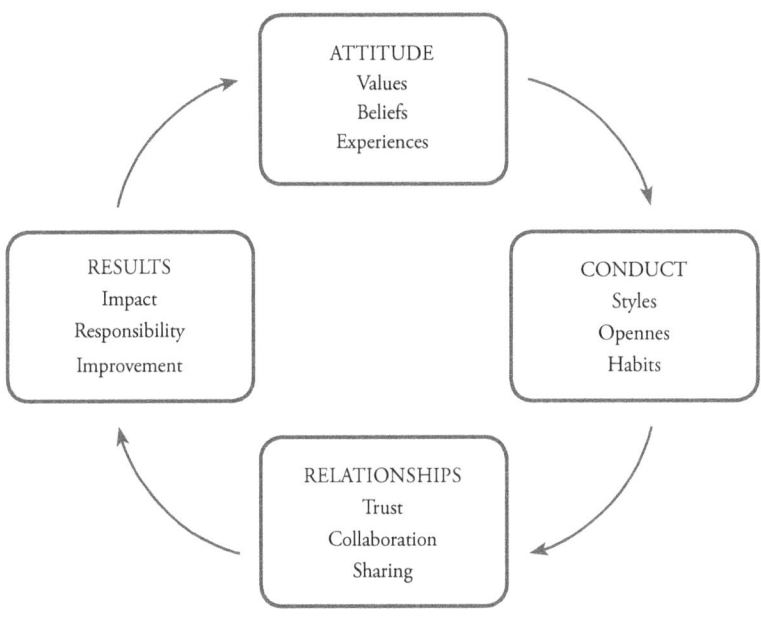

47   Crane, Thomas G. The Heart Of Coaching : Using Transformational Coaching to Create a High-Performance Culture.(2 ed.) San Diego California: FTA Press.

Your attitude reflects your way of thinking, and is the first step to lead you where you have never been before. Attitudes are formed in relation to the values, beliefs and experiences we have throughout our life. Attitudes help establish our behaviour and are sometimes called "hidden motivators" because they cannot always be seen. Thus, it is important to be careful of what is coming into our mind. Consider … how many news programs do you watch a day? What type of music do you listen to? What books, movies and TV shows are your favourites? If, during any given time, you realize that your attitude is negative and pessimistic with regard to life and your future, you should pray, seek advice and work on discovering the true reasons behind that attitude. The thoughts you keep in your mind affect your short- and long-term decisions. Every action is born from a thought. Watch your thoughts. All thoughts are born from the heart; therefore, guard your heart!

IT IS THIS SIMPLE!

I once read an article about why there is such a gap between developed and underdeveloped countries. This article evaluated three different variables to analyse if these contributed to the development of the countries. Here are the three variables:

The first variable they analysed was the age of the countries. After examining countries such as India and Egypt, the idea was ruled out because these millennial nations are still at a low level of development.

The second variable analysed was constituted by natural resources available in developed countries. But after analysing nations like Japan, a world economic power, with such a small and irregular territory (not suitable for agriculture or livestock), it caused serious doubts in the minds of researchers. The Japanese territory is like a large floating factory that imports raw material from all over the world, processes it, and the resulting product is also exported to the whole world accumulating wealth. We also studied the case of Switzerland. It does not have cocoa but produces the best chocolate in the world. In its few square kilometres, the people breed sheep and cattle, and cultivate the soil for only four months in the year, since it is winter the rest of the year. It has the best quality dairy products from all over Europe. Like Japan, it does not have natural products but provides and exports quality services that are very difficult to overcome. It is another small country whose security, order, and work turned it into the 'bank of the world.' These examples definitely inspire us and let us know that the natural resources which a country can have are not those that determined the level of development.

The third variable they analysed was the intelligence of the people. But after a series of studies, it was identified that this does not make the difference either.

Then, they reached the conclusion that it is the attitude of the people that makes the difference–their attitude towards work, the future, the way they spend and save their money; their attitude towards justice and the type of authority with which they lead the country; their love for education, for freedom and for God. Their attitude is what influenced their lives, and your attitude will also influence your life and that of your family.

I once read a very interesting story that I would like to share with you:

> There was once a young man who left his hometown to go looking for new experiences in life. This young man went into a new city, and saw an old man sitting on a bench. As he passed by, he asked the old man, "Hey, how are the people in this place?" The old man answered, "What are the people like in the place where you came from?" The young man replied in a bad way, "The people from the

place I come from are naughty, vulgar, insensitive, moody, and I just couldn't live there anymore! That's why I came here." The old man replied, "Well, that's what you'll find here." The very sad young man bowed his head and kept walking. He was hoping to find something different.

Soon after, another young man arrived under the same circumstances as the first. In search of new adventures, he arrived in the city and saw the same old man sitting on the same bench. Then, he asked the same question, "Hey, how are the people in this place?" The wise old man replied again, "How are the people where you came from?" The young man responded enthusiastically, "The people from the place I come from are affectionate, kind, and helpful. It is a pity that I had to leave!" The old man replied, "Well, that's what you'll find here." The young man happily continued on his way.

Another man who was sitting next to the old man, and who had seen both young men ask him the same question, was intrigued and asked him, "Excuse me, sir, how is it possible that to the same question you gave two such different answers?" The old man replied, "I answered both the same... because what they have inside is, what they will find outside."

Our attitudes have a direct impact on how we interpret reality and get results. Who we are inwardly has a profound influence on the way in which we face life and the possibilities we have to succeed.

If we start a business thinking that we are going to go wrong, not only will we have to fight against life and against the challenges that lie ahead, but we will also have to fight against ourselves!

Our winning attitude, however, should not come from what we can do on our own strengths. It must be rooted in what God has done and can do through us.

QUESTIONS AND PRACTICE FOR CHAPTER 4

1. God longs for us to enjoy Whole-life prosperity, and He gives us the talents and skills we need to discover and flourish. Write down the talents and abilities that you possess, and then highlight or emphasize those you must develop more.

    _____

    _____

    _____

2. Our attitudes determine our conduct. The values, beliefs, and experiences determine how you will act. This will influence your relationships and affect the results of everything you plan for yourself. So, analyse and observe your attitudes and conducts, and write down those you need to reinforce because they are positive (+) and those you should modify because they do not benefit you (–).

    _____

    _____

    _____

3. Read the following truths. Then plan to think about and meditate on them for the next forty days. We will remind you at the end of the next chapters.

- I am the daughter of the most-high God. (John 1:12)
- God is my Father, and He wants what's best for me. (Matthew 7:9-11)
- I am beautiful and wise because He has made me beautiful (Genesis 1:31) and His Spirit gives me a special wisdom that is not from this world. (James 3:17)
- God has not given me a cowardly spirit, but one of power, love and self-control. (2 Timothy 1:7)
- I was designed to win, to defeat. Defeat sin, defeat death, defeat Satan, and prosper by my endeavours. (2 Corinthians 2:14, Psalm 20:7-8)
- Everything that happens to me is for a reason. God can transform my defeats into victories. (Romans 8:28)
- There is no safer place in the universe than the one I will find in the middle of God's will. (Ephesians 1:11-12; Colossians 1:9-10; Hebrews 13:20-21)

Chapter Five

LEARNS TO WORK WITH HER HANDS

DR. NILDA PÉREZ

"She keeps herself busy making wool and linen cloth."
Proverbs 31:13

For a Woman Who Prospers, working with her hands is a pleasure because she does so, not only with diligence, but also with good will, knowing that her efforts are well spent. She does not do things out of compulsion, but because she wants to. Her motivation is the love she has for her husband, her children and her home, so she feels happy doing it.

Working with your hands means working with what you've got. It is our duty and responsibility to identify which are the things that God has placed in our hands and that we can use to move forward in our financial life. In the Biblical passage of the widow and Elijah, the prophet asks this lady a question that she was not expecting; "Tell me, what do you have in your house?"[48] That is why it is important

---

48   2 Kings 4:1-8,

to put whatever you have at His disposal. The Lord can take that and multiply it greatly. His command brings into being what did not exist.[49] He created the universe with the power of His Word and can create in you and for you whatever He wants.

The parable that Jesus tells in Matthew 25:14 teaches us that God gives each person different abilities and talents. Some even have more capacity or ability than others, but God gives something to everyone. This parable clearly shows that it is our duty and responsibility to multiply what God has given us. Some use what God has given them to glorify Him, but others ignore their relationship with God and the talents they were given. The first two servants received different amounts, but both were faithful to properly utilise what they had been given by the Lord. The third servant did not develop what his master had delegated to him, and therefore it was taken from him and was given to those who had used the resources well.

Woman! It's time to multiply and develop what God has given you. A lot or a little, put it in His hands. Do not limit yourself, because you are capable of doing great things to glorify the Name of God.

For many years, I have worked as a consultant in organizational development and as a certified coach to help large companies. I would like to give you five recommendations for you to enter into a continuous growth process:

1. Know Yourself
2. Discover Your Passion
3. Look at Yourself In the Mirror (seek "feedback")
4. Develop Your Creativity
5. Establish Goals

---

49   Romans 4:17

1. *Know Yourself*

The Woman Who Prospers is the one who is aware of her strengths and of the areas that need improvement. So, she works with her strengths and seeks help for her weak areas. Know yourself in depth and learn how to properly handle your feelings and impulses.

I recommend that, each week, you look for an inspiring and welcoming place where you can reflect on how it went during the week and identify how you can improve what you are doing. In order to improve our skills, it is extremely important to be aware of the areas that we need to optimize.

Now, I would like to share with you what they call a "SWOT Analysis" (Strengths, Weaknesses, Opportunities, and Threats) in the field of strategic planning. This analysis leads you to identify internal factors (strengths and weaknesses) and external factors (opportunities and threats) that can influence the prosperity of your personal and family life.

This self-test is a very good tool that is usually used in companies. However, in analysing this material from James Manktelow, I found that it can be used on a personal level. Below you will see this theoretical theme in more detail, and at the end of the chapter you will put it into practice.[50]

Identify your strengths

When you think about your strengths, think about those specific areas where you have been successful. Think of the skills others recognize in you. You can also think about that action of which you are proud. You can ask your family and friends what they see in you as strengths.

---

50   Manktelow, James. Personal Development Plan Work: Essential Skills for an Excellence Career. Mind Tool Ltd. 2007.

Consider:

1. What advantages do I have over the other people in the same line of business?
2. What makes me better?
3. What special or low-cost resources do I have access to?
4. What is it that others see in me as strengths?[51]

Years ago, people looked at their strengths and weaknesses. Then they focused on "balancing" their strengths, working on their weaknesses. However, I recommend you focus on your strengths and not emphasize your weaknesses. Look for people who are strong in your weaknesses and who complement you. In that way, you can create a team of people in which everyone works in their strong areas (like a football team). This will be a real winning team!

Identify Your Weaknesses

To identify your weaknesses, you have to be as honest as possible. You should think about those areas where you feel vulnerable and do not have enough experience, but which are important for your development.

Consider:

1. What can I improve?
2. What should I avoid?
3. What characteristics of my personality do people perceive as a weakness?
4. What things in my character reduce my possibilities of growing financially?[52]

Be honest with yourself. Remember that the more aware you are about these areas, the greater opportunity you will have to work on

---

51   https://en.wikipedia.org/wiki/SWOT_analysis
52   Same as the previous one

them, improve them, or ask someone to help you in order for you to be able to focus on your strengths.

Identify Your Opportunities

To identify your areas of opportunity, you can look around and identify the specific elements that can help you to be successful. Think how you can maximize your strengths and minimize your weaknesses. In which areas can you see a greater growth opportunity?

Consider:
1. What do I have in my hands? What has God given me?
2. Where can I put my capacities into practice?
3. Where is there a need for product or services?
4. What is the need for the product or service that only I can satisfy?

Identify Your Threats

To identify your threats, think about those things that can cause you worries or stress. Identify which skills are key to continue with your development and which are the things that you still need to improve.

Consider:
1. Which obstacles am I facing?
2. What is my competition doing?
3. What are the things that could bring me to a complete halt?
4. How vulnerable am I to the lack of money?

2. Discover Your Passion

People can do a job because they need it to live, to earn money, or out of fear for reprisals. However, people give their lives for a passion. Think, for example, of the martyrs of the faith or the leaders of the independence movement of your country. Although their mission may not have brought them fame or fortune, they were willing to put their lives at stake. The passion they felt for that vision and mission mobilized them.

Consider:

1. What do you truly enjoy doing with all your heart?
2. What kind of things would you do all day without getting tired?
3. What type of activity gives you energy?

Probably what you love doing, is where God has given you the gifts and talents that will make you prosper. I read somewhere that one should ask, "What are the things that make me angry?" In the answer to that question lies the problem that God wants you to solve in the world.

Sometimes women tell me that they do not feel talented, that they have not had the opportunity to study a profession, that they have never felt successful in anything in life. Some have even suffered mistreatment from their husbands who degrade, humiliate, and despise them. So it is time for you to reject all those ideas and start seeing yourself as God sees you. He has created you in His image and likeness. He has given his own Son for you. You are the most valuable of the universe to God.

The key to working with excellence is to work wholeheartedly and put passion into what you do. Passion is total dedication, devotion and commitment; it is the first step towards realising your goals, it increases your willpower, and makes the impossible possible. Here lies the great difference between a leader and an ordinary person. A leader is characterized by her passionate attitude toward her life and work, and her genuine desire to achieve goals no matter how complicated the road ahead may seem to be. Therefore, if you want to be a prosperous woman in your family, in your business, in your city, and in your country, I encourage you to work with all your heart and with all your strength in everything you undertake.

3. *Look at Yourself In the Mirror* (seek "feedback")

None of us would go out into the street without first looking in the mirror, would we? The truth is that some of us love to look at ourselves in the mirror, in the windows of houses, at the shops, in car windows ... and on anything that reflects our image! That is precisely the idea of "feedback." It is to see in others how we are reflecting in them. The information we receive from others will lead us to make internal adjustments that modify our behaviour.

If we are on a stage about to deliver a speech and the audience is looking at us and they begin talking to one another and they start to smile, we will immediately look to see if we do not have something hanging from our hair or if there is something weird in our dress. That's why we pay attention to what the audience tells us in response to our behaviour. Try to understand how it impacts their lives and what we should do differently to better communicate or to sell ourselves or whatever we present better.

Feedback is a very important process because it helps you to raise awareness of the behaviours you have but do not see. There are areas that we cannot see ourselves and we need the help of another person to let us know "the good, the bad, and the ugly" of our behaviour. Ask yourself honestly and listen carefully.

Consider:
1. Do I have a nervous tick that distracts people?
2. Do I talk too much?
3. Do I explain myself clearly, or confuse people?
4. Do I stand correctly?
5. Is my dress appropriate, or distracting people?

One final warning: we should not confuse feedback with criticism. Criticism is always negative; it is an attack on the person, focuses on the problem, and addresses past actions. Feedback has a positive goal, focuses on future action, on the solution, and presents creative alternatives to create a better future.

Below is a scheme from Kurt Wright's outline of the differences between criticism and feedback:[53]

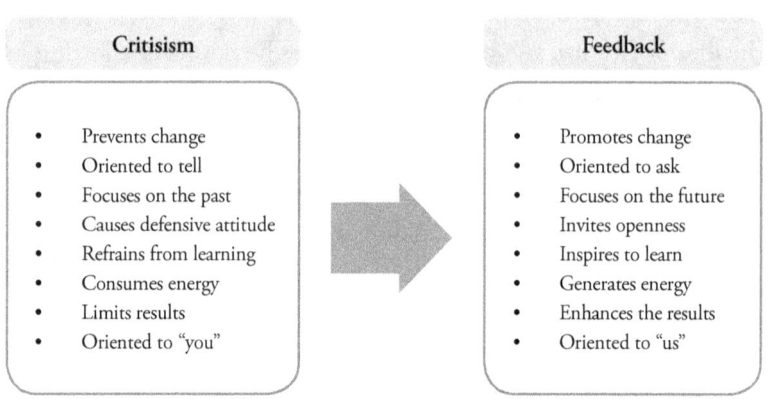

Critisism	Feedback
• Prevents change • Oriented to tell • Focuses on the past • Causes defensive attitude • Refrains from learning • Consumes energy • Limits results • Oriented to "you"	• Promotes change • Oriented to ask • Focuses on the future • Invites openness • Inspires to learn • Generates energy • Enhances the results • Oriented to "us"

4. Develop Your Creativity

Being creative is risking being adventurous, daring, and providing alternatives for solving difficult situations. To be creative, we must sharpen our imagination and go beyond reality and develop our talented productivity. To be creative is to accept that sometimes the most absurd ideas develop the best products and services.

In 1968, Dr. Spencer Silver, a scientist from the 3M Company, mistakenly created a "failed" glue that did not properly attach one paper to another. Instead of throwing the formula into the trash, he began to think how to use it creatively. In 1974, his colleague and friend Art Fry came up with the idea that the paste was good for keeping in place pieces of paper that he used to mark in the church hymnal the hymns that the choir would sing. Thus, the "Post-it"®

---

53   Wright, Kurt (1998) *Breaking the Rule: Removing the Obstacles to Effortless High Performance*. CPM Publishing. Idao.

notes were born—one of the most famous and successful products of the 3M company with sales that have reached a billion dollars annually![54]

Dewitt Jones, a renowned National Geographic photographer, defines creativity as the ability to observe the ordinary and see the extraordinary,[55] and he states: "When you come into the world with a sense of abundance rather than scarcity, you feel more and more comfortable when changing the problems into opportunities by finding new angles and coming to the same elements from a completely different direction".

Richard Florida, a university professor, was the first to coin the term of the 'creative class,' referring to the working class who, with their good attitude, developed their talents to produce innovation.

In these times of crisis, it is important to generate creative ideas that allow us to be effective and look for economic alternatives to move forward. There may not be many jobs available, but there is a lot of work that can be done.

Creativity is the process of clearly presenting a problem in the mind (either imagining it, visualizing it, supposing it, meditating, contemplating it, etc.) and then originate or invent an idea, concept, notion or outline according to new or unconventional lines. It involves study and reflection rather than action. We are living and working in the knowledge era, in which the most important thing is to generate new ideas.

The most prosperous cities in the world are also the most creative. So, do not limit yourself and develop your creativity. God is a creative God and has given you and me the ability to be creative women.

---

54   http://archives.secretsofthecity.com/magazine/reporting/features/twenty-five-years-post-it-notes-0
55   Jone, Dewit. Every Day Creativity: Preview Guide.

5. *Establish goals*

Succeeding depends largely on establishing goals and striving for them. The famous king David had as a goal the construction of a magnificent temple for God and carried out all the plans and the necessary preparations for his son to carry out the project. The temple of Solomon was a project that lasted two generations before it materialized.

The key is to set goals that are specific, measurable, achievable and realistic, and which can be reached in a certain time. (This concept comes from the acronym S.M.A.R.T. A synonym for the word 'smart' is intelligent.)

Goals give us:
- Direction
- Meaning
- Motivation
- Energy
- Satisfaction
- The opportunity to learn and move forward in life

Dwight D. Eisenhower, former President of the United States, once said, "A plan is nothing, but planning is everything." What does this mean? It means that the only way to achieve any goal is to work with discipline until you achieve it. There is an exercise at the end of the chapter for you to practice this.

THE WHEEL OF LIFE[56]

The Wheel of Life is a graph that is used to represent how a person's situation is valued in different areas of life. For each area, there is a

---

56   Institute For Empowerment Coaching (2003). 151 Rte. 33 Suite 240, Manalapan, New Jersey, USA. Training Manual: Module I.

valuation from 0 to 10 which depends on the current situation of the person. Upon completion of the evaluation, a score is obtained and then evaluated to analyse how to reach the optimal situation. In the wheel, the eight areas of life are identified, which every person must order and balance to maintain a productive and effective life.

These eight areas are:
Personal development; Spiritual Awareness; Fun and Enjoyment; Intimacy and Social life; Health and Aging; Personal finance; Career and Profession; Family and Parenting.

I invite you to do your self-assessment. In each of the categories, you will assign a value from 1 to 10 where 1 is the lowest value and 10 is the highest. Then, make a circle for each score and join those circles with a line. This will allow you to see which category is most lagging behind and to which you need to pay more attention in order to thrive in a balanced way. This wheel shows that one cannot advance in his/her life at a rate of continuous growth if it is unbalanced in some of the areas. Once you identify which areas of your life you need to focus and work on, develop an action plan for improvement. I recommend that you look for a person who can help you think about how to grow balanced in your life. It can be any leader, counsellor or professional mentor.

In conclusion, when you set goals both in your personal and in your business life, you must do it in a way that helps you fulfil them and not to frustrate you. For that, I invite you to apply this model to your own world.

Let's see below each of those characteristics that correspond to the letters that make up the acronym SMART.

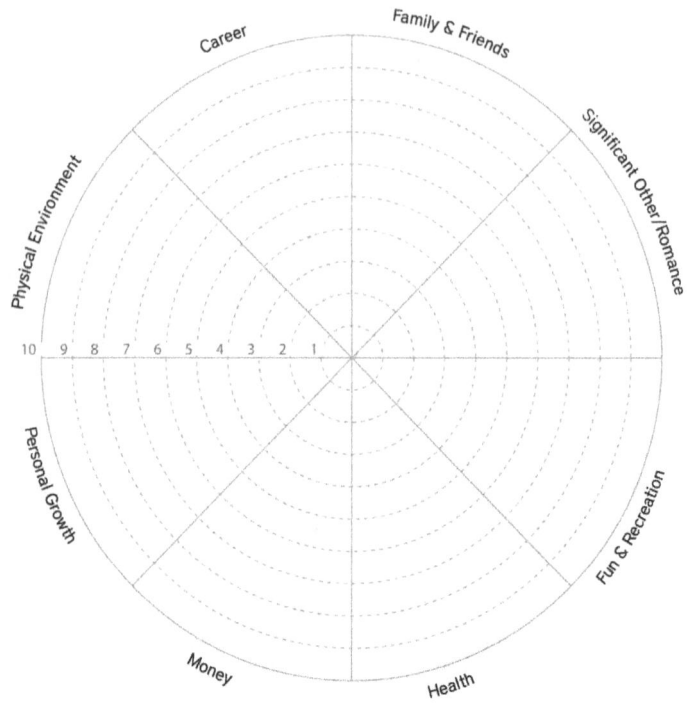

Specific: the more specific the goal, the greater the probability to be able to accomplish it. Describe your goal clearly by answering these questions: What do you want to accomplish? Where? When and how will the situation change?

For example:

General declaration of the goal: I want to improve the finances of my home.

Specific declaration of the goal: I want to save x amount of money in order to invest in a new business that will be a new source of income for our family.

Measurable: When you set a goal, you should always have a way to measure whether you are achieving it or not. You cannot improve something that is not measurable. As Latin American women, we do not like to measure. But if we don't measure, we don't know where we stand. When our children have the flu, the first thing we do is find a thermometer and measure their temperature. Once we measure, we know what to do. The same goes for your goals. You must have goals you can measure.

Example:

General declaration of the goal: I will start saving money.

Measurable declaration of the goal: In the next six months, I will save 10% of my net available income in order to save approximately $ 2,000 that I will use to start a business.

Achievable: Make sure the goal is within a reasonable limit that is achievable.

Example:

Declaration of an unachievable goal: Despite earning $500 a month, I will save $5,000 in the next 6 months.

Declaration of an achievable goal: Since I earn $2000 per month, I will save $2,000 during 6 months setting apart $12 per day.

Realistic: Is this a realistic goal for you? Be conscious about your limitations and capacities. Make yourself goals that you can reach in a reasonable manner. Do not set unrealistic goals—they just bring you frustration.

Example:

General Declaration of the Goal: If I manage my money well, next year I will not have debts and I'll be able to have an emergency fund that will cover the expenses for a six-month period.

Realistic Declaration of the goal: If I manage my money well, next year I'll have an emergency fund that will cover at least two months of expenses and I will have paid off two of my four credit cards.

Time: You need to set a time limit for your goals. Many women want to find work outside their home or want to begin a new business. However, if you don't set a date to do it, time will go by and the goal will not become real. Having a time set will push you to fulfil this goal.

Example:

General Declaration of the Goal: I will save more.

Declaration Determined in Time: I will start next month, and I will save 10% of my available net income every month, and by December 31, I will have $3000 in my savings account in the bank.

QUESTIONS AND PRACTICE FOR CHAPTER 5

1. Complete the following chart, and you will be able to identify and evaluate your strengths, weaknesses, opportunities and threats. Do you think you know yourself well?

Strengths	Weaknesses
_____	_____
_____	_____
_____	_____

Opportunities	Threats
_____	_____
_____	_____
_____	_____

2. What is your work passion?

_____

_____

_____

3. What differences are there between feedback and criticism?

_____

_____

_____

4. How can you develop your creativity in the environment in which you are working?

_____

_____

_____

GUIDELINES FOR SETTING YOUR GOALS

Here are some types of goals that a young person might be interested in establishing in different areas of life. I suggest you complete them with your own goals.

Art/Music/Creativity: What goals do I want to accomplish for the development of these areas in my life?

_____

_____

_____

Education: Where do I want to be in ___ years with regard to my education? (Specify the amount of time)

_____

_____

_____

Relationships: For the next three years, how do I want my relationships to be? Do I want to have more friends? Spend more time with the family? Have a better relationship with my mom or dad? Get married? Continue being single?

_____

_____

Spiritual: What type of spiritual growth or commitment do I see for myself in the upcoming years?

_____

_____

Sports/Physical Condition/Health: If I am successful, how would I like my health or physical condition to be in a couple of years? ____

_____

_____

_____

Work: In which direction do I see my future professional career progressing?

_____

_____

_____

Now I invite you to make a list of the dreams that you have in your heart. Write them down in the following four groups:

My dreams:

Personal: What are my personal dreams?

_____

_____

_____

Professional: What do I dream I could achieve with regard to my work/business?

_____

_____

_____

Family: What would I love to see in my family?

_____

_____

_____

Spiritual: How should my relationship with God be?

_____

_____

_____

Identifying your goals, dreams, and desires will provide you with a clearer picture of what you want to accomplish in life. Once you have established goals, assess them according to the wheel of life.

NOTE:
Remember that you should continue with the task of item 3 that you began in Chapter 4.
(Biblical declarations to think during 40 days)

See page 99

Chapter Six

LEARNS TO VENTURE INTO THE BUSINESS WORLD

DR. NILDA PÉREZ

"She keeps herself busy making wool and linen cloth."

Proverbs 31:13

As women in Latin America, we need to break with the idea that the business world is only for men. Sexism has penetrated deep into our Latin American countries, and we need to change the way men and women interact in business life to be able to free us from financial slavery. As men and women, we must work together, shoulder to shoulder, to build a better future for our families and for our country. We must abandon the belief systems imposed on us by the culture in which we have grown, and change these into new beliefs that come directly from the Word of God. We are what we think and think what we believe. I will share with you a chart that I have drawn up. You can see that to enter the world of business, you must also know and evaluate the things that need to change.

Self-Awareness and Evaluation

Nancy Leigh de Moss wrote a book called, "Lies Women Believe: And the Truth That Sets Them Free." Here I share with you some of these beliefs accompanied by comments about the truth that sets them free.

The lies...	The truth that makes you free...
I am not worthy.	God created the universe and saw that it was good. Then He created man and, finally, He closed his creation process with His ultimate work of art - woman. Your worth does not depend on what others think of you. It depends on what God thinks of you. You have been created to the image of God, you are the closest to God there is in the universe. (Genesis 1:26-27).
I need to learn to love myself.	We already love ourselves. If your goal is to learn to love yourself, you'll end up selfish and self-centred in your own life. What you need is to learn to forget yourself (Matthew 16:24) and embrace the unconditional love of God for you. The problem is not that we have a 'deficient self-esteem, but that we have a 'deficient image of God.' He loves you unconditionally and nothing else matters in the world. "Who, then, can separate us from the love of Christ? Can trouble do it, or hardship or persecution or hunger or poverty or danger or death?" Romans 8:35
I cannot change the way I am.	Sure you can change...whatever you want! Galatians 2:20 says that when Jesus comes to live with us, we die, and He starts living in and through us. We stop being like our family or the way we were in the past and we are completely transformed. (Romans 12:1, 2). We take on the character and behaviour of Jesus.

I don't have time to keep all my commitments.	In John 17:4 Jesus told the Father: "I have finished the work You gave me to do." In barely three years of ministry, Jesus completed His task successfully. The reason? Focus. The Lord completed the job that God wanted Him to do, not what the disciples or the people of Israel wanted him to do. You have all the time in the world to finish the work that God wants you to do, but if you try to satisfy and please others, you will never have enough time. Focus!
A career outside the home is worth more and is more satisfying than being a wife and mother.	Read Genesis 2:18 and 1 Timothy 5:9-10. There isn't a more precious calling than the calling to be an instrument of God to give life to our children and take care of our family. There is nothing wrong in working outside the home, or less honourable to work at home.
I need to get married to be happy.	Read 1 Corinthians 7:32-40. Happiness is a status of the soul and does not depend on the things you have … such as, a husband.
I cannot control my feelings.	Philippians 4:19 says, "My God will supply your needs." John 14:27 adds, "Do not be worried and upset." Philippians 4:16 affirms "Don't worry about anything." Isaiah 26:3 declares, "You, Lord, give perfect peace to those who keep their purpose firm and put their trust in You." and 2 Corinthians 10:5 continues saying, "we take every thought captive and make it obey Christ." Every time you feel your emotions betray you, seek strength in the Word of God. Take your 'captive' thoughts to the Word of God.
If my circumstances were different, I'd be different.	Your identity is in Christ. It doesn't matter what circumstances you are in. The old is gone, the new has come! God can change your circumstances.

It's unfair to suffer.	Suffering in a Christian's life has a reason. to make you stronger. God perfected Jesus Christ through afflictions (Hebrews 5:8), and He wants to perfect you through the 'gym of life' that will allow you to be more perseverant and perfect. Read James 1:3-4 and 1 Peter 5:10.
I cannot take it anymore.	Every time this thought comes, repeat to yourself the same words in 2 Corinthians 12:9: "My grace is all you need." What you need isn't more strength, more patience, more intelligence or more work. What you need is more of God's grace. One day in His Grace is worth more than a thousand days of work.

Many times we believe things that are not true but have been told to us since a young age, "You are good for nothing." "You never do things right." However, the mighty Word of God tells you, "Anyone who is joined to Christ is a new being; the old is gone, the new has come."[57] It doesn't matter who you were in your past. God has made you a new person. Reject all the nonsense you have been told as a child and say with the apostle Paul: I can do all things through Christ who strengthens me!

Having faith when we see our economic situation stagnant or declining is a challenge. But putting faith in our Almighty God can move the mountain of doubt and fear. Change your way of thinking to change the way you live. Having faith means learning to rest in the power of Jesus Christ, and not on your own strength. Do not worry, better yet, let your Heavenly Father know all your needs and expect the impossible from Him.

I would like to share with you the story of entrepreneur Cony de Morales, a prosperous Guatemalan woman who entered the

---

57   2 Corinthians 5:17

business world after spending 26 years working as a housewife. Cony learned to change her way of thinking and has let herself be used powerfully by God.

> "My husband, a very visionary and hard-working businessman, always longed to have a wife in his home to care for and bring up his children. But life often gives us surprises, and unexpectedly, at age 59 my husband died from a sudden heart attack. Three months after his passing, I had the courage to go to the cemetery; I felt lonely, empty, helpless, and although surrounded by many people, loneliness and insecurity tormented me. I did not understand why this situation had happened to me. I was the youngest of my sisters and had three children. At that moment, I cried out to God in despair. I opened my Bible, and guided by the Holy Spirit, my eyes rested on the words of Isaiah which said, "Do not be afraid, you will not be confused...because your husband is your Maker, the Lord Almighty is his name; and your Redeemer ... because the Lord has called you as a woman abandoned and sorrowful in spirit. For a brief moment I left you, but I will gather you with great mercies...and all your children will be taught by Jehovah and the peace of your children will be multiplied."[58]

These words gave me the courage to face life and my circumstances; that He would allow me to live and realize that I was not alone. He was giving me a purpose for life, both for me as well as for His children, and then the Lord continued to tell me: "Enlarge the place of your tent, stretch your tent curtains wide ... lengthen your cords, strengthen your stakes."[59]

---

58   Isaiah 54: 4-7, 13
59   Isaiah 54:2

I certainly faced very difficult situations that I had not encountered while my husband was still alive. I went from being a housewife to managing the legacy of my husband. Overnight I became father, mother, and executive of our company with the support of my children. God helped me at every moment, bringing out in me gifts and abilities that I had not discovered and started to put them into action. He has covered me with a cloak of wisdom and authority, by grace, to face the unknown world of business.

I encourage every woman who is facing loneliness, widowhood, divorce, abandonment, and also single mothers because, my friends and sisters, we are not alone! God has promised to be our husband, helper, counsellor, and defence counsel.

If our lives depend on Him, we will be more than conquerors because we have been created to be victorious, and we are right in the very centre of God's heart. Let's seek His face, His will, His wisdom, and His intelligence to be women of victory even in the midst of all circumstances."

Just as Cony, you too can also face the challenge of becoming a successful businesswoman. Let me share with you some recommendations on how to enter the business world:

1. Honestly seek the will of God for your life.
2. Plan challenging expectations, but make them realistic and achievable.
3. Take advantage of the opportunities that come your way.
4. Master the art of improving yourself continuously.

Fundamental Guidelines for Venturing into Business

The importance of discovering and developing God's purpose for us will help us feel secure, useful and active to serve and make a difference in the lives of others. When there is purpose, life has meaning. On the other hand, when setting goals for your business life and persevering to achieve your goals with excellence, you'll face your challenges, maybe with many problems and frustrations; but you will find creative solutions for each of them. We will always experience successes and failures. The secret is to endure, to be patient, and endeavour to accomplish your goals. If you want to fulfil God's purpose for your economic life, you must;

1. Work hard.
2. Manage yourself with excellence.
3. Be patient and persevering.
4. Take risks.
5. Make sacrifices.
6. Tolerate frustration.

1. **Work hard:** The true winners are those who, at one point, have been willing to do things that most are not willing to do. They are the ones who are always willing to travel that extra mile that is almost always necessary to succeed. Join this group of women.

2. **Manage yourself with excellence:** Start looking for ways to continually give more than what is expected of you. Push yourself to do more than the average person. God wants you to work with excellence.

3. **Be patient and persevering:** Get rid of excuses and affirm with determination because "if God is with me, no one can be against me."

4. **Take risks:** As women we always tend to look for quick and easy solutions although they are generally not the best options to take. Television and advertising promote that world, where everything is "light" because it costs little effort and places us in what is called our "comfort zone," where we feel comfortable, where we know and control everything, and where there are no challenges. However, it is important to realize that any goal and objective that is truly worthwhile will take us out of that comfort zone.

5. **Make sacrifices:** It means giving up one thing in order to obtain something better. It is very true that nothing can be gained without any effort or without dedication; however, when you are in the business world, it takes a greater effort to get what you want. We will have to wisely evaluate which things are priorities and define which ones you need to "give up."

6. **Tolerate frustration:** Understand that at times (more than you'd think) things will not go as you want them to go. You should not be crumbled by this. You need to develop that tolerance to face life successfully, and avoid anger or depression causing misfortunes.

   Self-awareness and character development are the core of our personal development, not just as leaders, but also as women of spiritual prosperity.

A study, from the Harvard University, affirms that 85% of the performance of the leaders depends on personal character. Thus, we must work on our being. In the business world, being is more important than doing.

God made us women with special characteristics. For example, He has provided us with the ability to multi-task. The virtuous woman described in the book of Proverbs does not only take care of her house, her husband, and her kids, but also has other interests and activities. She is an administrator, a businesswoman, makes wise decisions, is prudent, and earns good money. The Woman Who Prospers exercises good stewardship, and plans and organizes her work well. She assumes great responsibilities, and she can trust that she will be able to face any situation with excellence because her trust is put in the Lord and not in her own abilities.

Dr. Dick Wynn, former president of Youth for Christ, used to say, "God can use anything that we make available to Him. He does not look at our ability, but rather our availability." When a young boy came to Jesus and gave Him some bread and fish, He fed thousands of people. The disciples had a serious budget deficit and underestimated what the young boy had brought, but God appreciated it greatly and used it for His glory.

Consider: What can you put at the Lord's disposal? Can you sew? Can you cook? Do you collect antiques? Do you like flowers, photography?

Talking about flowers…I would like to share with you the true story of Celene Peña, a beautiful woman of God who has developed a very thriving business in the flower industry in the United States.

Celene is mother to two girls and a boy. One of her girls has an intellectual disability. Celene had in her heart the desire to help her husband with the family's finances. Their financial situation was not good. One afternoon while listening to a radio show and desperate about their financial situation, she decided to call the show for more information. At the show, they gave her the phone numbers to call the Compass office. She diligently called the ministry offices where she was listened to, and then sent some material for her to begin to make her budget, and they prayed for her. At the time of her call, they mentioned that Dr. Andrés Panasiuk would be offering a workshop on how to successfully manage family finances from a Biblical perspective in the city of Houston.

Celene decided to attend this conference with an open heart. She was willing to receive and obey whatever would be said in the conference because she was convinced that the message would come from God. She believed in the teachings and made them part of her life.

Beginning the journey toward financial healing was not easy, it was a process. However, she was willing to take the first step, which was to placing a shoe box in her kitchen and put all the receipts from that month in it. This was her first step to train and discipline herself little by little in the area of finances.

She also listened to Dr. Panasiuk say that God can use anything that we offer him, including a hobby or something we like doing. Celene thought at that time that she liked flowers and that, maybe, God could use her passion to start a business.

Despite not having a lot of capital–just $200–Celene began her floral business. With time, God blessed her with a contract in Washington DC to make 800 flower arrangements for a national convention. Not many years later, God once again opened doors that she would never have dreamed of, when she received a contract for the preparation of the flower arrangements for the "Super Bowl" of the National Football League (NFL) in 2003.

Together with that opportunity, she was also presented with a great challenge: How to deliver the floral arrangements without messing them up or seeing the flowers wilting? Willing to work with excellence, Celene asked God to help her...and one night at 3 a.m., God woke her with an idea in her mind. She did not want to miss this opportunity, wrote the idea down, developed it, and then patented it.

This is how she invented a mechanism to load big amounts of flowers without wilting them. This invention has been considered as one of the best inventions in the floral business.

In the year 2003, her business was nominated by television chain Univision and the Hispanic Chamber of Commerce in Houston, Texas as "The Emergent Business of the Year." In 2004, the Microsoft company chose her as a fine example of an SMB (Small and Medium-sized Businesses) in the United States. For this recognition, she was given computer equipment, free training, and they published her story on the Microsoft webpage.

The success that Celene experienced was due to her putting what she had into the hands of God: A deep love for flowers. God took this, plus her adherence to the financial and business principles of the Bible, and God opened doors and opportunities where there were none before!

God did it with Celene, and He can also do it with you!

QUESTIONS AND PRACTICE FOR CHAPTER 6

Exercise a) Discover the way you think with regard to life. Answer these questions:

1. What is the first thing that comes to mind when you think about a business?

    _____

    _____

    _____

2. What are your feelings about money?

    _____

    _____

    _____

3. What is your greatest fear when you think about starting your own business?

    _____

    _____

    _____

4. What do you really think is the purpose of money?

_____

_____

_____

5. How do you measure success?

_____

_____

_____

6. How dependent are you of another person in relation to money? If you are dependent, how do you feel?

_____

_____

_____

Analyse the answers you wrote to know what your belief system is and the paradigms that guide your behaviour. If you want to prosper and develop, you need to identify and reject your "limiting beliefs" and replace them with Biblical principles that reflect a clear image of yourself. This is the key for developing your potential.

Exercise b) After having answered these questions, analyse yourself and identify the ways you limit yourself. For this, please fill in the blank spaces.

Ways I limit myself (lies I have believed)

1. _____

   _____

2. _____

   _____

3. _____

   _____

"We learn to fly only in direct proportion to our determination to rise beyond doubt and to transcend our limitations." David McNally.

Exercise c) Here is an exercise that will help you overcome the barriers to establish a formal commitment with your future of success. Answer the following questions with honesty:

1. What are some barriers which can stop me from having a full commitment to accomplish the goals I have?

   _____

   _____

2. What steps can I take to overcome these barriers?

_____

_____

3. Specifically, to what am I committing (in time, money, other resources) in order to make this goal come true?

_____

_____

These questions will guide and help you develop the character that God wants you to have. Through the advice of the mother of King Lemuel, God shows us that the Woman Who Prospers is a woman of firm character, great wisdom, many abilities and great compassion. The Woman Who Prospers is a woman that participates in productive activities, helps provide for the welfare of her family and above all, complies with the will of God for her life.

NOTE:

Remember that you should continue with the task in item 3 that you began in chapter 4 (Biblical declarations to think about for 40 days).

See page 99

Chapter Seven

LEARNS TO SAVE, IS AN INVESTOR AND SO MUCH MORE

DR. NILDA PÉREZ

A Woman Who Prospers is a woman who is always ready for the unexpected things which life throws at her. Many times, our financial problems did not begin because we spent more than we should. They began because "something unexpected" happened that needed that extra expense. I want to emphasise that "the unexpected would not be so unexpected if we were waiting for it!"

In the financial area, the only way to do this is to save and reserve money for the unexpected. We should be cautious women, and have an emergency fund in case of an unexpected event that could arise at home. Unexpected expenses not only cause bitter disappointments, but also can cause a high level of pain and frustration if people don't have the money to cover such expenses.

The Woman Who Prospers not only puts her money to work, but also saves it regularly. The parable of the ant[60] tells us, "Lazy people should learn a lesson from the way ants live. They have no leader,

---

60 Proverbs 6:6-8

chief, or ruler, but they store up their food during the summer, getting ready for winter."

Saving is foreseeing a future need. Saving is storing whatever will be needed to satisfy that need. Then, we won't need to ask others. Saving is having foresight, it does not mean we are a provider. Remember, God is our Provider. Our task is not saving to provide for our family (that is God's job). Our task, as faithful administrators[61] to save in preparation for unexpected situations in the future.

Saving does not mean stockpiling but reserving for future needs. The difference is the attitude that the person has with regard to the saved money, not the amount. Everyone can save. It doesn't matter if you earn much or earn little.

Here are some examples of ordinary people who saved big sums of money:[62]

The Rev. Vertrue Sharp planted hay, tended cattle, was a preacher and a teacher. Meanwhile, he saved every cent he earned. When he died in 1999, he left an inheritance of two million dollars to the Children's Hospital in East Tennessee, the University of Tennessee Medical Center, and other charity organizations. Truly, a minister rich in money and in character as well.

Roberta Langtry was a school teacher who earned a very modest salary in Toronto, Canada. However, she always lived a very simple life and invested part of her money, month after month and year after year, especially in stock of technology companies, banks and insurance companies. When she died in August 2005, she had an accumulated wealth of $3.800.000 – which she left as a gift to several charity organizations in her home country.

---

61   1 Corinthians 4:2
62   http://www.thedigeratilife.com/blog/index.php/2008/03/10/serious-savers-who-died-very-wealthy/

Mary Guthrie Essame was a retired nurse who lived in an old Victorian house, and who wore used clothes and old shoes all her life. Her neighbours were surprised when they learned that her estate was $10.000.000 when she died in January 2002. (The money was designated to many charity organizations.)[63]

To begin saving, you can put into practice a well-known mathematical formula; the '80-10-10 formula. This means that every month you take 10% of your income and give it to God, save another 10%, and learn to live on the remaining 80%. The question now is, "How much should I save up?" The ideal is to save between two and six months of expenses (depending on the country, and your position in the company). This way you will be prepared for any contingency or emergency. Remember what the Proverb says: "The wise have wealth and luxury, but fools spend whatever they get."[64]

Saving is easier when you have clear goals. So the first thing you need to do, is identify why you want to save. You need to save for an 'emergency fund' first. For example; such an emergency fund can be 50% of the monthly expenses of the family. Once you have that, you should establish a reserve fund for the family (3 or 4 months of family expenses). Finally, you can establish certain saving goals for example to buy a house, for retirement, for paying your studies or your children's education, or for vacations.

Once you have enough money in the bank and you have reached your saving goals, you don't need to continue saving. Now you can invest that money in more important things, like helping others or supporting God's work around the world.

---

63   http://en.wikipedia.org/wiki/Roberta_Langtry
64   Proverbs 21:20

Useful ideas about saving

Giving before saving

For our heart not to become greedy, we need to be generous while saving. I would like to suggest that we ask ourselves the following questions to better organize ourselves financially and start saving:

1. Do you tithe and give offerings?
2. Do you have a budget?
3. Do you write down your expenses?
4. Do you spend less than what you regularly earn?
5. Do you shop compulsively?
6. Do you have an emergency fund?
7. Do you have a habit of saving?
8. Are you generous to give and make sacrifices for God's work?
9. Do you have a retirement plan?
10. Do you generate any income through small or medium size businesses?

I also invite you to answer these questions to be able to evaluate how well organized you are in the financial area. The way we handle our money is an external expression of an inner spiritual condition.

1. Save regularly: There are people who ask me if they can save while they are in debt. My answer is a complete YES! It is important to save even if it is only very little at a time, because it teaches us to develop a habit of saving. One of the biggest problems we have in Latin America is that we have not been taught to save regularly. We need to be wise women who teach these habits to our children as well.

2. Establish a fixed percentage for saving: Get used to save at least 5% of your available net income. Increase your percentage as you adjust your budget and get out of debt – without falling into greediness and selfishness.

3. Here are some possible goals in regard to saving:

- Short-term saving goals
  - For an emergency fund
  - To buy appliances
  - To go on vacation
  - To give us "a luxury"
- Long-term savings
  - For a business fund
  - For retirement
  - To leave some money behind for our children and grandchildren
  - For major purchases (housing, car, etc.)

Here is a revolutionary concept: Once you have clearly defined your goals, these should also become your limits. If you do not put limits on your standard of living, you will go through life never having enough. The Bible speaks clearly against greed. Jesus told the following story:

> "There was once a rich man who had land which bore good crops. He began to think to himself, 'I don't have a place to keep all my crops. What can I do? This is what I will do,' he told himself; 'I will tear down my barns and build bigger ones, where I will store the grain and all my other goods. Then I will say to myself, Lucky man! You have all the good things you need for many years. Take life easy, eat, drink, and enjoy yourself!' But God said to him, 'You fool! This very night you will have to give up your life; then who will get all these things you have kept for yourself? This is how it is with those who pile up riches for themselves but are not rich in God's sight" [65]

---

65   Luke 12:16-21

The problem with this rich man was not the amount of money he had accumulated as a result of his work, but in that he wanted it all for himself. We need to reflect and ask ourselves: How much is enough for me? With how little am I willing to live? What do I do with the excess? When should we stop running after material things and be content?

Answer the question: What are my dreams? How much is enough for me?

_____

_____

Let me share with you the answers Latin American women gave me when they answered what their dreams were:

✓ A house
✓ A car or means of transportation
✓ Education for their children
✓ Their own education
✓ Insurance coverage
✓ Health insurance
✓ A business of their own
✓ Be free from debt
✓ Travel
✓ Regular vacations
✓ Entertainment (favourite sport)

What is the maximum level that you are aiming for in your financial life? How much is enough? A house? Two cars? Food? An investment for the future education of your children? At some time should stop, because if we don't, we will fall into what we call the "A-little-bit-more syndrome".

Do you know how this syndrome works? When they asked Rockefeller, the multi-millionaire, how much was enough for him (as being the richest man in the world), he looked at the reporter and said, "Just a little bit more." Money never satisfies. We need to learn to get rid of the 'a-little-bit-more' syndrome and write our goals on a piece of paper. This way, when you reach that financial goal you can gladly say, "We've made it! We've reached our goals. We can thank God and be satisfied!"

So, write down the goals that you have set for your life (the list you previously made). Make two copies of this list, one to put on your bedside and the other to put on the refrigerator door or on your bathroom mirror. You need to be reminded regularly where you are going in life. Having specific goals is also a good way to set financial limits, to set aside energy and resources for other causes. This type of attitude will not only provide us with a deep material satisfaction (by having reached our goals) but also a deep emotional and spiritual satisfaction. This is the main idea behind the concept of Whole-life Prosperity.

She is a real estate investor

She looks at land and buys it,
and with money she has earned she plants a vineyard.
Proverbs 31:16

Real-estate purchases are a long-term investment strategy. Generally, properties tend to gain value over time. Although not always the case, as we have seen with the 2008-2015 global economic crisis, in which properties dramatically declined in value. But despite this situation, it is not the norm, and it may be expected that properties will grow in value. Real-estate represents safe investments in the long term. Therefore, we recommend that if you and your family have not purchased a property, you start thinking about doing it.

In Proverbs 31:15 we see an example of how this woman uses her wisdom to make this type of investment. Let's look at the steps she took to purchase this property.

First, she appraises and evaluates what she is going to purchase before taking a decision. When we make a big investment, like the purchase of a property, we must apply wisdom and prudence. We need to analyse and study the property to be purchased. Here is a summary of some key points I recommend prior to purchasing a property:

1. Make an analysis of the budget
2. Confirm your credit record (Good credit)
3. Seek out a loan and compare several offers
4. Make a list of the negotiable and non-negotiable items
5. Make your first "property inspection" to know the different alternatives.
6. Take your time to look at options and thus be able to make a decision that you feel satisfied with. However, do not stress trying to see everything that's for sale. Be sure to prepare a good selection before going out to visit.
7. Try to understand if you are making a good investment regarding a future sale.
8. It will surely be hard to find a property that meets 100% of all the elements you are looking for, you will need to decide what aspects matter the most.

While it is necessary to take into account all these aspects, do not undervalue your first impression about a place. Sometimes we fall in love with sites that have nothing to do with our original idea or the advantages we had studied.

She is an entrepreneur who plants a vine and begins a business

She looks at land and buys it,
and with money she has earned she plants a vineyard.
Proverbs 31:16

The Woman Who Prospers is one who is brave, and strives to realise the purposes of God in her life. To be an entrepreneur means to begin something, to take initiative and be proactive. The entrepreneurial woman is characterized by an active and positive spirit that leads her to assume risks and commitments while trusting in the promises of God. Being entrepreneurial requires growth and development in leadership, your relationship with God and in the authority delegated to you, by Him. Be brave and courageous women, willing to win the good fight.

Carrying out entrepreneurial activities is not easy; it requires widening our inventiveness and creativity. It also implies trusting God completely and facing the challenges and adversities with determination and courage. Such courage is an inner strength that helps us fight for what we consider to be worthwhile.

You might have a great idea in mind and are asking yourself, "Where do I begin?" Something that can help you get organized and develop your vision of the business you want to carry out is a 'business plan.' With it you'll be able to evaluate the strong and weak points of your dream and be able to take the most effective decisions to work with them.

KEY POINTS OF A BUSINESS PLAN

1. A description of the business that explains

    b. The characteristics of the business: describe the business, the services you will offer, where it will be located. What is the vision, the mission and purpose of the business? Identify what needs your business will address. Then describe the name of the business, the location, the licenses, permits and other requirements.

    c. The operational structure: Answer the following questions: How is the business going to operate? What do we need in terms of personnel, and equipment?

        Often, we want to begin a project but don't have the slightest idea of what we need to do in operating the business. I recommend you investigate and interview people who have had similar businesses. They can help you understand its operational aspects.

    d. The products and services you will offer: Make a detailed description of the services and products you'll offer. Highlight the benefits the clients will have when acquiring this service or using the product and how this will meet their needs.

    e. The price list: in order to price your services or products, is important that you research how a similar product sells in the market. Remember that you will not set the price, the customer will. The price always ends up being established through 'the law of supply and demand.'

2. Market research:

    This study can give you an idea about the chances for success or failure of your business project and help you develop the strategies to sell and promote your product. Additionally, it provides you with information about consumer habits and to whom the product and/or service is directed at. Even if yours is a complex market in which expert professionals work, you can carry out a simple market research by making a survey using key questions that can help you clearly define the main characteristics of the market you want to reach. It is imperative to define its potential, characteristics and purchasing styles, their consumption levels and preferences. If you want to sell coffee to office workers, you will do better downtown, where there are more offices, than in the suburbs; and probably, you'll sell more in the morning than at noon. You will need to find out what types of coffee to offer and at what prices.

3. Sales strategy:

    Once you know your market through the market study, you'll be able to develop a sales strategy. In the global and competitive markets we live in, it is not simply selling a product or service at a low cost, but selling a quality product or service which is different and offers accessibility to the customer who is willing to pay a reasonable cost to obtain this product or service. Nowadays customers are well informed and better equipped to make purchasing decisions. Therefore, the sales person should be better prepared and show credibility, security and trust in whatever she is selling. When we talk about sales, it is important to establish and maintain relationships with the customers for the long term. It has been proven that customers buy from sales persons they trust. The customer has very high expectations and expects knowledge and ability from the sales persons. Here are some very practical sales strategies

    a. People don't buy products or services, they buy solutions for their problems; therefore, describe the unique advantages of your products or services.

b. Highlight the successes achieved by your product and support such affirmations with facts and testimonies of satisfied customers.

c. Convince your customers that your product or service will allow them to improve their business.

d. Motivate your customer to decide and close the sale.

4. Financial projections: It is important that you are able to make daily, monthly and yearly projections of your sales. You should forecast as real as possible taking into consideration the income from the sales to the customer and all operational costs. Here is an example of elements to be considered in the budget of a business.

BUDGET		
Category		Balance
Sales Income		$ 103.269,50
Operational Costs		
Salaries	$60.667	
Rent	6.859	
Insurance	720	
Transportation Expenses	5.557	
Material and equipment	2.400	
Office equipment	1.200	
Printing	1.800	
Electricity	1.068	
Water	132	
Telephone	596	
Cell phone	754	
Internet	170	
Mail	720	
Trips	960	

Total Operational Costs	$ 83.603	
Net income		$ 19.666,50
Tax Payment	$ 7.017,50	
Final net income		$12.649

She is a Fashion Designer and Decorator

"She makes bedspreads and wears clothes of fine purple linen."

Proverbs 31:22

The Woman who Prospers is finely dressed. This does not mean that she dresses from a boutique and buys expensive gowns, but that she is well dressed, decorously, fine and beautiful. She is conscious about her influence, and dresses to the standards of her leadership. She certainly knows that outer beauty is important, but the most important is the inner beauty that can only be provided by God.

This verse refers to the fact that she is also a tailor, in other words she like to decorate her home, her business and her belongings. As women, we have a special gift of making things beautiful and lovely.

I learned that God is a God of order, so our home should be one that is orderly, clean and well decorated. It should be a cosy place where our family feels at home and we can live well. Always strive to provide your family with a comfortable, cosy and tidy environment.

She is an Owner of a Micro enterprise

Nowadays, advances in the technology and access to the Internet make it possible to work from home. The office at home is a new concept that has gained popularity due to the great amount of people working from there. Working from home provides us some flexibility and freedom.

Having a home business also means that you can organise your time as best suits you. Time is maximized, there is probably less travelling to do, and being at home we can reinforce family ties, which are fundamental to our life, and therefore, for the success of everything we do. Studies highlight how important participating in the activities with the children is for family stability and to enjoy a better family and social life.

However, to be successful in your micro-enterprise, managed from home, requires a lot of discipline. Discipline is the driver of every project. Respecting rules and times are key habits for the success of any business project. A good leader develops the discipline that their collaborators will also respect.

If you are going to own a small business and work from home, it is imperative to emphasize the importance of time management. Time is your most valuable possession, and how to use it will decisively influence your performance. The great dilemma that many of us face is that we have too much to do and insufficient time to complete them.

GUIDELINES FOR SOLVING PROBLEMS IN THE RIGHT ORDER

One of the greatest dilemmas concerning time management is to face the decision of choosing between what's important and what's urgent. If we don't know how to manage or organize our time well, we will make the mistake of responding to urgent activities that are not necessarily important.

Important things are those that add and contribute to your life project. These things are usually done in the medium and long term. The urgent, on the other hand, demands that you attend to it immediately! If you have planned your time, this urgent thing might not actually be important, and you will be able to dedicate this irreplaceable resource to what will give you more dividends.

Classify the problems the problems you will have to solve this day and solve them in this order:

Urgent and important
Important but not urgent
Urgent but not important
Neither important nor urgent

Here is a chart that exemplifies this:

		YES IMPORTANT	NO
URGENT	**YES**	• Crisis • Projects with a deadline • Problems and pressure <div align="right">1</div>	• Interruptions • Useless calls • Upcoming matters <div align="left">3</div>
	No	<div align="right">2</div>• Preparation • Building of relationships • Clarification of values • Life plan	<div align="left">4</div>• Reading Junk Mail • Trivial things • Time wasters

FEAR OF FAILING?

Cynthia Kersey, in her book "Unstoppable", gives us a challenge: [66] "Who is telling you that you cannot begin your own business? Your own family? Your friends? You can, if you want. You have all the potential to become a businesswoman. Don't give up, give yourself the chance to be successful."

---

66   Cynthia Kersey. Unstoppable. Sourcebooks, Inc. pp 139-143

How about these 'almost never happened' stories
..

"Stop your business right now and get back what money you can. If you don't, you'll end up without a penny in your pocket." The lawyer of the now-famous billionaire Mary Kay Ash told her this just weeks before she launched her first cosmetics business.

"You have a nice voice, but it's not that special", Diana Ross was told by a teacher while being rejected (she became a famous singer) during an audition for a musical from her school.

"I had failed on an epic scale. An exceptionally short-lived marriage had imploded, and I was jobless, a lone parent, and as poor as it is possible to be in modern Britain, without being homeless. The fears that my parents had had for me, and that I had had for myself, had both come to pass, and by every usual standard, I was the biggest failure I knew." J.K. Rowling. Coming out of this failure stronger and more determined was the key to her success.

Oprah Winfrey, one of the most successful individuals of our time, grew up in sheer poverty. Born to a single-mother living on welfare, her upbringing was wrought with pain and anguish. She was physically, mentally and sexually abused during her childhood. She ran away at thirteen-years of age and got pregnant at fourteen-years old. But she later lost the baby shortly after birth. She was also fired from her first job for being unfit for television.

Have you ever been so afraid of failing at something that you decided not to try it at all? Or has a fear of failure meant that, subconsciously, you undermined your own efforts to avoid the possibility of a larger failure?

J.K. Rowling says, "It is impossible to live without failing at something, unless you live so cautiously that you might as well not have lived at all, in which case you have failed by default."

Many of us have probably experienced this at one time or another. The fear of failing can be immobilizing – it can cause us to do nothing, and therefore resist moving forward. But when we allow fear to stop our forward progress in life, we're likely to miss some great opportunities along the way.

It's important to realize that in everything we do, there's always a chance that we'll fail. Facing that chance, and embracing it, is not only courageous – it also gives us a fuller, more rewarding life.

Remember God will empower you! "For the Spirit that God has given us does not make us timid; instead, his Spirit fills us with power, love, and self-control."[67]

---

67   2 Timothy 1:7

QUESTIONS AND EXERCISES FOR CHAPTER 7

1. What is the most important thing you need to do to develop the habit of saving?

2. What are your savings goals?

3. How will you try to get your whole family to learn the principles of saving?

4. What guidelines do you consider important when owning your own business?

5. Write in here things you consider important and which you consider urgent. Then analyse and write how you are going to resolve them.

NOTE:

Remember that you should continue with the task in item 3 that you began in chapter 4 (Biblical declarations to think about for 40 days).

See page 99

Section Three

The Woman Who Prospers impacts the next generation and blesses the needy because she has given herself to God.

How hard it is to find a capable wife!
She is worth far more than jewels!
She brings home food from out-of-the-way places,
as merchant ships do.
She is generous to the poor and needy.
Her children show their appreciation,
and her husband praises her.
He says, "Many women are good wives,
but you are the best of them all."
Charm is deceptive and beauty disappears,
but a woman who honours the Lord should be praised.
Give her credit for all she does.
She deserves the respect of everyone.

Proverbs 31:10, 14, 20, 28-31

Chapter Eight

INFLUENCES AND TEACHES HER CHILDREN

DR. MELVY DE LEÓN

"Her children show their appreciation,
and her husband praises her."
Proverbs 31:28

A song from famous Guatemalan singer Ricardo Arjona about women expresses, I don't know who invented them, I don't know who did us this favour, it had to be God".

It definitely had to be God. Women can be found everywhere. You go to an office, and who greets you there? The female receptionist. You go to school, who receives you there? A female teacher. You go to a hospital, and who greets you there? A female nurse. What is the first word babies learn? Mom. When they get up, who do they call first? Mom. When they want to eat who do they ask for something? Mom. When they cry, who do they look for? Mom.

THE SCOPE OF YOUR IMPACT

The woman who wants to impact the next generation is positive, optimistic, sure of herself, and someone who enjoys her role in life. Proverbs 31 emphasizes three specific areas where she takes care of her family because she feeds them, she clothes them and sets a good example.

"She keeps herself busy making wool and linen cloth.
She brings home food from
out-of-the-way places, as merchant ships do.
She gets up before daylight to prepare food for
her family and to tell her servant women what to do.
She doesn't worry when it snows,
because her family has warm clothing."

Proverbs 31:13-15, 21

These passages talk about the woman who doesn't mind getting fatigued in order to fulfil her duties as a housewife, and does so willingly. She does not eat the bread of idleness (v. 27b). She uses her time well, so she doesn't miss a minute. When night comes, she lights her night lamp for the chores inside (verse 18). She sleeps only as much as necessary and gets up very early, when it is still dark (v. 15) so she can prepare breakfast for the family and servants, and assigns each servant the work they must do in the day.

She is not one who likes to spend the evening playing cards or attending a society dance. She looks around for wool and linen (v. 13), in order to obtain the best in quality and price, and to work it with her own hands (v. 19), not only for family clothing (v. 21) but also for the needy (verse 20). She doesn't think that, by doing that, she has lowered her dignity or status. The spindle and the wheel are mentioned here in honour of her, while the ornaments of the daughters of Zion are mentioned in Isaiah 3: 18 for their dishonour. She does not only undertake those tasks that can be carried out in the peace of her own home and seated in a chair, but she also undertakes other tasks which require all her strength (v. 17). For example, she does everything possible so that the family finances go well. From a merchant ship (v. 14), she gets the necessary supplies, so that neither hunger nor famine takes her by surprise.[68]

I have always been impressed by the way women feed their children. From the very moment of conception, the placenta is formed from the same cells that form the baby, it gets attached to the wall of the mother's uterus and forms connections with the mother's blood to provide the baby with oxygen and nutrients. The placenta also forms connections with the foetus's blood to remove waste, which pass into the mother's blood, and then to the mother's kidney to be eliminated. The placenta also protects the foetus from many harmful substances and microorganisms.

This connection remains forever in the relationship between a mother and her children, not only in the very fact of feeding them, but in providing care, protection and love. We must keep open communication with them because many times we are their only hope to bring them back to a balanced life in the different stages through which they pass. This communication must be honest, sincere, and transparent.

However, there are adults who want to appear to their children as something they are not. They pretend to make them believe that they never experienced the struggles that they are having, that they never fell in love, or were weak and that is why their children do not come to them.

In my work with teens and young adults, I once asked how many trust their mother and have her as a friend. Only 2 out of 10

---

68   Commentary to Proverbs 31. Taken from "Exegetical-Devotional Commentary to the Whole Bible." Poetic Book – Proverbs Book 2. Editorial CLIE. cristomeama. blog.com.es/2007/01/31/comentario_a_ proverbios-1654438/ - and similar pages.

answered that their mom is their best friend. We are in the 21st century and many mothers still have taboos of talking about issues such as dating, sex and friendship with their children. In the next few paragraphs in this book I would love to encourage you to reverse the numbers. Start by approaching your children with a sincere heart. Overcome your own taboos and start a sincere and empathetic dialogue that allows your son or daughter to say everything that lives and feels in their lives.

> *"Teach children how they should live,*
> *and they will remember it all their life."*
> Proverbs 22:6

How do we teach our children?

1. With words, Never forget these commands that I am giving you today. Teach them to your children. Repeat them when you are at home and when you are away, when you are resting and when you are working." Deuteronomy 6:6-7

Those of us, who are mothers, need to be up-to-date with the news and with the modern world. We constantly need to be reading books and magazines of current topics such as art, music, science, finances, culture in general and technology.

We now have the possibility to look for articles on the Internet, and transfer this knowledge to our children. We should spend time talking to our children. We must learn to communicate with them on a deeper level than the rest of the world. However, the essential element is to know the Holy Scriptures because this will help us to teach the eternal truths to our children. Things like love God, love your neighbour, parents, relevant friendships, dating, sex, finances, studies and work. In this way we can transmit Christian values essential to their lives.

2. By Example, And you should imitate me, just as I imitate Christ." (1 Corinthians 11:1)

We cannot teach what we don't live out. We need to be consequent in all areas of our lifestyle. A teenager approached my husband one day and said, "Good message Pastor, I just hope you live what you taught us!" Young people expect to see in us good manners worth imitating. The famous professor Albert Einstein used to say, Giving a good example is not the most important way to influence others, it is the only way of doing it".

> One mother brought her son before Mahatma Gandhi and begged, Please Mr. Gandhi, tell my son not to eat sugar." Gandhi, after a brief pause answered, "Bring back your son to me in two weeks' time". Two weeks later, she returned with her son. Gandhi looked directly in the eyes of the boy and said, "Don't eat sugar." Thankful but perplexed the woman asked, "Why did you ask me to wait so long? You could have said the same thing two weeks ago!" Gandhi answered, Two weeks ago, I was also eating sugar".[69]

We cannot ask our kids to do things if we, as mothers, are not willing to lead by our example. In his book, "Why do teenagers rebel?" Dr. Luis Palau says that teenagers rebel because of the hypocrisy of adults, and I agree with him. We think our children don't notice, but they do! And they just laugh at us behind our backs, because they don't dare to tell us our failures. Hence, I urge you to imitate Christ, so that our kids see in us the character of our Saviour!

3. With their participation.

Children should be part of the things happening in their family environment. If there is a victory in the family, the kids should be part of it. If there is a crisis, the children should know about the

---

69   https://preilly.wordpress.com/2008/07/19/gandhi-story/

situation. How are we going to prepare them to face life if we don't allow them to see how we resolve the problems of adulthood? Kids need to grow, mature and understand the reality of life within their families. They need to know that there are good times and not so good times in life. They need to be part of the process of living as a family in order to be prepared to lead theirs. An open and honest dialogue within the family creates an environment where problems are discussed and explained. It creates a proper environment for them to participate according to their age and comprehension level.

What are we teaching our children?

"Teach children how they should live,
and they will remember it all their life."
Proverbs 22:6

TO LOVE GOD.

"What does the Lord your God require of you? He requires only that you fear the Lord your God, and live in a way that pleases him, and love him and serve him with all your heart and soul" [70]

If you have a personal relationship with God, if you are a daughter of God, your children will be impacted for your love to God. When our children are no longer by our side, we will have the confidence of knowing that wherever they go or are, the love of God will remain with them.

The opportunities we have in life are one-of-a-kind and we should take full advantage of every moment to teach them about the love of God. Dr. Andres Panasiuk and singer/songwriter Miguel Angel Guerra wrote a devotional for fathers and daughters entitled

---

70   Deuteronomy 10:12

"Butterfly Dreams". My husband used to have a regular devotional with my daughters using this book. I recommend it.

Even though the book is oriented to fathers and their daughters, I also took the opportunity to read them this 30-day devotional. They loved it and, even when they knew the stories by heart, they enjoyed it as if it were the first time they read it. Then they would tell me, "Mommy, give me a butterfly kiss". (A "butterfly kiss" consists of passing my eyelashes over their cheeks, blinking my eyes; this was tickly. Try it with your kids!)

ABOUT SEXUALITY

Are you afraid to discuss this with your children? Don't worry; you're not the only one. Unfortunately, I did not have the privilege of talking to my mother about such interesting topics as these, or even being allowed to ask questions about it. It was 'not done!' A few days before I was getting married, my mother asked me, "Daughter, why don't you tell me about personal things?" I smiled slightly; it was a question I wanted to hear many years ago, and at that very moment I decided that this would not be repeated with my daughters. I confess that it hasn't been easy, but I've had the courage to face their questions and respond honestly. I've had the opportunity to teach them topics that many children do not dare to talk to their parents. Often, they made me blush, but I thank God that they have talked to me about their concerns.

I would not like that another girl their age be the one to teach them. I would not like it to be a magazine or a TV show, or even the Internet. I want to have the privilege to do it myself.

One of my favourite counsellors during my teenage years was Dr. Luis Palau, who has influenced many young people. The frank and open way in which he approaches this subject in his book, "Sex and Youth" makes you see sexuality from another point of view. I recommend that all parents have in their library a useful consultation tool where they will find guidelines which will help guide their children in the way of life, love, sex and marriage. How often will we neglect this important issue? I would like to share some practical ideas for those of us who have the privilege of being mothers, grandmothers or aunts to help the next generations to deal with their worries.

Young people today know too much about sex. They know more than you and I have ever learned together in our entire lives. We live in a culture obsessed with sex, and that obsession is exploding to damage our society. Advertising companies take advantage of this interest to sell their products. They use sex to sell cars, alcohol, clothes, bathing suits, perfumes and even food! That is why the youth of yesterday and today both have a misconception of the meaning and value of sex.

The first step we must give as parents is to overcome the fear of talking about the issue with our children and, especially for us moms, as we spend the most amount of time with them. We need to return to the principles and values found in the Bible, the Word of God. Moms, we must break with the premise that sex is dirty and ugly, or a taboo, so I encourage you to read your Bible where you will get the guidance you need.

If you want a passage about the beauty of love and the purity of marriage, read the book of the Song of Songs in the Bible. If you want to know the most powerful warning I have ever read against sexual immorality, look for Proverbs Chapter 7. If you want instructions regarding the order of a happy, ideal and wonderfully Christian family, read Ephesians chapter 5. If you long to know the destiny of those who mock a pure life that pleases God, read 1 Corinthians chapter 6 in detail. If you want to see an example of how God blesses a young man who remains pure despite having terrible sexual temptations, read the life of Joseph in the book of

Genesis chapter 39. If you want to contemplate the punishment of a nation because of its depravity, read the story of Sodom and Gomorrah in Genesis chapter 19.

If you want your children to live a happy and productive life, it will depend on the orientation that you provide as a mother. Guide them to believe in Jesus Christ and begin today!

ABOUT FINANCES

Teach the next generation about finances. We should avoid that they make the same mistakes we made. The question sometimes is: At what age should we begin to teach them?

I believe that since the age a child starts counting, they can learn basic things about the management of money. You'll be surprised of the capacity a 5-year old has to learn about these matters.

1. We should teach them about giving generously

    "Honour the Lord by making him an offering from the best of all that your land produces."[71]

    Our daughters' birthdays (fortunately for us) are celebrated in the same month. I remember that a few years ago, they were given so many toys, that we decided to go to a nearby town, found a church and invited several children from the neighbourhood. We asked our daughters to give away those extra toys as a way to teach them to share.

    The most important for us is not teaching our children to tithe, as an activity, but teaching them to be generous, as a lifestyle. If our kids learn the art of generosity since an early age, whenever they become adults they will give without a problem.

---

71   Proverbs 3:9

2. We should teach them how to save
    "Lazy people should learn a lesson from the way ants live. They have no leader, chief, or ruler, but they store up their food during the summer, getting ready for winter".[72]

    Savings must be accompanied by goals. When our daughters asked for a cell phone, we told them that it was not a necessity, and that if they wanted to have one, they had to work to buy it. So they did some house chores and we paid them for it. After a month, they had the money saved to buy the cell phone. We accompanied them to the store and bought their phone. After that came the typical question, "Who pays for the calls and data?" According to what they agreed, they continue to do chores at home to pay for their own "prepaid calling card".

    When they become adults and work, they will have acquired the habit of giving and saving, but they learnt to do it by establishing concrete goals in their lives.

3. We should teach them to spend wisely
    "Look after your sheep and cattle as carefully as you can, because wealth is not permanent. Not even nations last forever".[73]

    It is important that our children from a young age know that money is meant to serve man and not man to serve money. They must learn not only how to save, but also how to spend wisely. Teach them the difference between a need, a desire for quality, or just a desire. Share these ideas that have already been discussed in the book and teach them to your children. Explain these differences and you will be raising children who will not suffer most of the economic problems that families have today.

---

72 Proverbs 6:6-8
73 Proverbs 27:23-24.

4. We should teach them to avoid getting into debt
"Poor people are slaves of the rich. Borrow money and you are the lender's slave."74

One boy told his dad he wanted a toy car, but the money he had was not enough. The father warned him that the toy was poor quality and not worth buying. However, the boy insisted and told his father to give him the difference of the money he needed. Dad said, "Well, I'll loan it to you, but you're going to have to pay interest." The boy did not know what he was getting into; he wanted the toy and wanted it right now! The toy, of course, did not last for a week as the father warned. However, the child had to face a sad reality - not only did he not have his toy, but he still had a debt with his father! Here is a useful tip:

As parents we should never pay our children's debts, they must learn to pay them themselves. It's part of their maturing process. Most parents (especially the mother) want to avoid their children's suffering. However, suffering is a very important part of the process of maturity. Let's accompany them in their suffering, and don't prevent it. Even God doesn't do that to us!

5. We should teach them to work for their money
"Hard work will give you power; being lazy will make you a slave."75

Work is not the same as exploitation. In our Latin American countries, we see families who decide to have children so that when they are adults, these children will support them. In some cases the matter is even worse - they are put to work since they have to meet their personal needs. That is exploitation.

---

74 Proverbs 22:7
75 Proverbs 12:24

Teaching them to work for their money is to teach them responsibility. Children at a certain age can do home chores and parents could pay them for it. However, let's be very careful; there are tasks for which they should not be paid. For example, it is the children's responsibility to make their bed, order their clothes, clean their room, and do homework. But there are others that are not their responsibility such as: washing the dishes, doing some errands, helping with cleaning the house, washing the car, etc. For these activities, you should pay them a certain amount of money, always in multiples of three. Buy three piggy banks or take three jars and put a label on each one saying 'Give,' 'save' and 'spend.'. Your children can then divide the money they receive into three equal parts and put it into the jars or banks. Apportioning earned money is a fundamental and very important skill in successfully managing personal and family resources.

I recommend to you the Compass programmes, written by Howard and Beverly Dayton for your children. "Give, Save, Spend" for the 5-8-year-olds, "The Secret" for ages 8-12, and "Two Masters" for teens. You can never start too early, and it's never too late to teach your kids how to handle money – God's way!

Mothers will impact the next generation when we are present in their world. Make, the promise stated in Isaiah your own, "I will give water to the thirsty land and make streams flow on the dry ground. I will pour out my spirit on your children and my blessing on your descendants. They will thrive like well-watered grass, like willows by streams of running water."[76]

In the hardest moments of our ministry as mothers, when we feel that storms beat us mercilessly, and we do not know how to deal

---

76   Isaiah 44:3-4

with the problems with our children, let's hold on to this beautiful promise which will help us stand firm to impact their lives. It is very common, during our church prayer meetings to realize that a mother's request is always for her children... Yes: that is a precious gift that God has given us, and we must fulfil it with faithfulness!

On a trip, going to a seminar, we arrived at a hotel to rest. I had with me a book I've always wanted to read. It is entitled "The Emerging Generation"[77], written by Junior Zapata. As soon as I read the preface, it captured my attention completely. That very day I completely devoured the book. As a woman over forty, I may not agree with all the content that this author presents in his book. However, I identified with many of the things that my contemporary Junior writes about the need to break with prejudices and paradigms so that we can love and understand today's teenagers.

Maybe you are a housewife, a nurse, a doctor, an architect, a professional, an entrepreneur or a businesswoman. No matter what activity you are engaged in: I encourage you to know the world this new generation lives in. Children have different ways of communicating and you as a mother should look for the most effective way to do it.

My oldest daughter is a very communicative girl and talking with her is not difficult. She likes for me to respond to her concerns and I have had the beautiful privilege of being very close to her in all the emotions she experiences as a teenager. My second daughter, on the other hand, does not talk much at all. I was asking God to help me get closer to my daughter when, on one occasion when we were both on the Internet, we started to "chat" in such an open manner like we had never done before ... Now, sometimes we are even under the same roof, she in her room and I in the living room, we find ourselves chatting on the Internet!

---

77   Junior Zapata. La Generación Emergente, Editorial Vida, 2005. Pages. 33, 34, 36, 43.

If you are a woman who does not like using technology, I encourage you to make an effort and learn about it. It seems difficult, but it really isn't. You just have to persevere. If you do, you will learn about the world in which your children live. You can see the photos that they 'post on the web' and what activities your children do. You will get to know better the people you are relating to, and you can even begin to receive text messages!

Here are some very important questions:
- Do you know the world of the internet?
- Do you know which pages your children visit?
- Do you know the friends they chat to in other countries?
- Do you know and understand your kids' fashion?
- Do you know your kids' dreams?

It's never late too late to begin.

I met a mother who told me, I don't like all this stuff that my kids are going through, but I need to learn about the new technology; otherwise, I'm going to miss the opportunity to get into their world. One day I'll no longer be with them, or they'll not be with me. "

I'm not suggesting that you dress in the same fashion as your daughters, nor am I asking you to accept everything from your children without a word. I only ask you to love them, to be an example and to transfer to their lives the legacy of eternal truths. Listen to music with them, enjoy a movie with them, and in time, tell them the difference between good and evil.

QUESTIONS FOR CHAPTER 8

1. What is the learning style you are using with your children?

2. How are you teaching them to:
*   Love God?
*   Save?
*   Give generously?
*   Spend?
*   Work for their money?
*   Choose good company?
*   Understand the sexual roles?
*   Apply Christian values?

NOTE:

Remember that you should continue with the task in item 3 that you began in chapter 4 (Biblical declarations to think about for 40 days).

See page 99

Chapter Nine

IS A BLESSING TO THE NEEDY

DR. ANDRÉS PANASIUK

"She is generous to the poor and needy."
Proverbs 31:20

D o you like to travel? When I lived in Chicago, I had a privilege to visit the Museum of Natural History many times. It's a unique place in the world. One of the most interesting collections has approximately 90,000 butterflies. Some show a really impressive beauty. I can also recommend the "Butterflies of the World Museum" in my home city of Buenos Aires, Argentina. They have around 70,000 specimens.

However, there is a great difference between any butterfly from any of these two collections that you admire behind a glass in a museum and the ones you would see in the Butterfly Sanctuary of the National Museum of Costa Rica. These are alive and the ones in the musea are dead. This is the difference between a successful woman, who has simply accumulated a lot of money, and a woman who has learned to be prosperous in the area of her generosity;

the second has real life. As you change the paradigms of your life to prepare you for a fully prosperous life, you need to change the paradigm of generosity. The Word of God says, Be generous, and you will be prosperous. Help others, and you will be helped."[78] This is not a magic formula from the prophets of prosperity. Of course, to prosper, you need to do much more than simply give money to others! But a generous heart has what it takes to be happy. It knows how to live detached from material goods and value the important things in life.

I firmly believe that one of the main reasons God allows us to enjoy prosperity is to share it.

Whatever your financial position, I think it is very important that we learn to share our blessings. If we don't do it, we die a little at a time as a human being. We are designed to share the little or much we have; both the joys and the sorrows. Egoism or greed is not very fitting for our spirit.

This is one of the reasons, for example, why the Dead Sea (in Israel and Jordan) is literally dead. The Dead Sea is 398 meters below sea level and the Jordan River delivers over six million cubic meters of water to this sea. However, the Dead Sea has a problem; it only receives water, it never gives it. The water then stagnates and with the evaporation produced by the desert sun, its concentration of salt increases. The normal concentration of salt in the ocean is 2 to 3%, while the concentration of salt in the Dead Sea is 24 to 26%, plus magnesium and calcium. There is no life that can withstand this chemical pottage! The Dead Sea, with its 1,000 square kilometres of surface, is large, rich in minerals, and is probably the best-known sea in the world. However, it has lost its life. It is empty inside. Nothing lives in it. This teaches us that giving, after receiving, is a vital process in order to maintain the freshness of our heart.

---

78   Proverbs 11:25.

There are several principles that I believe are important to have in mind when giving and I would like to share them with you:

THE CHRISTIAN WOMAN GIVES FIRST OF ALL, TO HONOUR GOD.

The custom of giving to God and His servants comes from ancient times. In the case of Judaism and Christianity, it was at least since the time of the famous Abraham and Melchizedek (about 4,000 years ago)[79]. It is interesting to note that 'tithe' (giving a tenth part of something) precedes the Mosaic law. Tithing was adopted by Christianity under the 'time of grace' because it was not established as a condition for salvation, but because it basically shows an attitude of the heart – that you love God.

The famous King Solomon says so in one of his proverbs "Honour the Lord by making him an offering from the best of all that your land produces".[80] Note that the first word (an imperative verb, an order) is the word 'honour'. The main reason for the Christian to bring money to the church, is an inner attitude; an internal acknowledgement of the recognition that all things come from God, and that HE is the owner of everything you own.

THE CHRISTIAN WOMAN GIVES WITHOUT EXPECTING SOMETHING IN RETURN.

The attitude of giving lies in love, and this action does not arise from personal gain. St. Paul explains this attitude when he writes to the Romans and the Corinthians.[81] The Christian gives to God as a son gives a gift to his father.

---

79   Genesis. Capther 14, verses 17 to 20.
80   King Solomon. Book of Proverbs, chapter 3 verse 9.
81   St. Paul. Letter to the Romans, chapter 11, verses 34 to 36 and First Letter to the Corinthians, chapter 13

Let's reflect: As parents, when our child gives us a hug and a kiss, why do we want them to give it to us? Out of love or because they want to 'get something' from us? We surely want them to give it to us out of love.

The idea of a child who approaches his/her parents because they want to get something out of it is not nice. In fact, the concept of the child who shows affection to his/her parents because he has other 'interests' in mind is a rather unpleasant idea.

What I ask myself is: Why are we teaching our people to do just that? Why do we listen to so many television and radio preachers teach Christians to give their offering to God so God can give them ten times more?

In my humble opinion, we should be teaching our people to give for love, not out of self-interest. The Word of God is very clear about it. Paul said to the Corinthian church, I may give away everything I have, and even give up my body to be burned—but if I have no love, this does me no good".[82]

When someone is taught to give out of self-interest, the results are immediate. But such a person is of no use to God because that only produces greed. The problem is, that kind of teaching is a boomerang and flies back to hit us. When people who give 100 dollars do not get 10 times more in return, then they begin to doubt. There are preachers of financial prosperity who, unfortunately, encourage this and even claim that when the donor doesn't receive in return it is due to his own lack of faith.

This kind of teaching is telling me that the problem is not merely a distorted and semi-heretic teaching., but also induces believers to give even what they do not have! The people who fall into these religious traps are, in general, the people who most want to please God.

---

82   1 Corinthians 13: 3

It's true that the Bible promises that God will open the windows of heaven to bless us when we honour Him with the first fruits of our labour. It is an eternal truth.

Returning to the topic of our children, I can affirm that my children have no idea of the financial blessings that my wife and I have and have saved for them. In the same way, you and I have no idea of the blessings God has kept for you and me in the future (some material, some emotional, some spiritual). However, when we bring our tithes and offerings before Him, God wants us to bring them, not out of interest for those blessings, but simply to honour Him and love Him.

Rabbi Meir was once asked, "Why do the Scriptures tell us in some passages that our sacrifices are pleasing to the Lord while in others it says that God does not take pleasure from our sacrifices?" The rabbi replied, It all depends if, at the time of presenting his sacrifice, man also included his heart in that sacrifice."[83]

THE CHRISTIAN WOMAN GIVES VOLUNTARILY

Although it is customary in many religions of the world to specify the type of offering you are bringing before God, it is not the same with Christianity. At least, it should not happen.

The key teaching is given by St. Paul when he tells the Corinthians, "You should each give, then, as you have decided, not with regret or out of a sense of duty; for God loves the one who gives gladly."[84]

The Christian takes the concept of the tithe from Judaism but doesn't see it as a rule, a law or a goal to fulfil. He sees it as a beginning, as a minimum on which to build a life of surrender

---

83   From the Jewish religious tradition. Midrash, Baraita Kallah
84   Second Letter of St. Paul to the Corinthians, chapter 9 verse 7.
       Good News Translation.

to God and to others. It is interesting that even in the apocryphal book of Sirach it is said, " Be cheerful with every gift you make, and when you pay your tithes, do it gladly. Give to the Most High as he has given to you, just as generously as you can. The Lord always repays and will do it many times over.[85]

THE CHRISTIAN WOMAN GIVES GENEROUSLY AND SACRIFICIALLY

When Jesus pointed his finger at someone to use as an example in the art of giving, He pointed, amazingly, to a widow who had placed only a few cents in the offering plates at the entrance to the temple. The Lord emphasized this event and incorporated it eternally in the pages of the Scriptures because she gave all she had.[86]

This widow could've had all the excuses in the world to sit at the door of the temple, reach out and ask. She was a poor 'single mother', useless to the Jewish society. As to rights and social status, it was not the same being a widower as a widow back in those days. The Law allowed her to receive for being a widow and poor; however, this woman, instead of extending her hand to ask, extended her hand to give.

There is a very powerful reason for why she did it. This woman had something many of us are lacking today - character.

A good friend of mine says, "giving is a symbol of wealth, while asking is a symbol of poverty," and he was not talking about material wealth or poverty. She who has a mature character will also be generous because she has something to give and will give even if she thinks she can't afford it.

---

85   Sirach 35:9-11
86   Gospel according to Mark, chapter 12 verses 42 to 44.

The secret in this matter is not that we all give the same amount, but that we give with the same sacrifice.

THE CHRISTIAN WOMAN GIVES SECRETLY

In the Sermon of the Mount, Jesus tells His disciples, "So when you give something to a needy person, do not make a big show of it, as the hypocrites do in the houses of worship and on the streets. They do it so that people will praise them. I assure you, they have already been paid in full. But when you help a needy person, do it in such a way that even your closest friend will not know about it. Then it will be a private matter. And your Father, who sees what you do in private, will reward you"[87]

Humility is an important element at the time of giving to others. Let's practice it in the midst of the electronic and ostentatious society we live in.

THE AMOUNT IS REALLY NOT IMPORTANT

As we previously said, the amount or percentage of money is not really important when giving. Some can give more, others less. What really matters is our 'inner 'being' and not our 'outer doing.'

Many times, I have encountered people who ask me if they should tithe, that is, giving 10% of their income to the church. There are two things that I regularly answer.

Firstly, I say, For this matter, obey your pastor and spiritual leaders and, if you agree to be part of that community of faith, you should follow their leadership." Secondly, I generally clarify that, in ancient times, the people of Israel did not give 10% of their annual income to the temple. They gave more. This attitude only shows how little

---

87   Gospel according to Matthew, chapter 6 verses 2 to 4. Good News Translation.

we know Scripture and why we do the things we do.

Allow me to explain: ancient Jews had only one annual harvest; however, they gave three tithes - two annual tithes and a third one every three years. The first tithe was to be stored in the temple.[88] The second one was for the widows and orphans of the Hebrew people.[89] The third tithe (every three years) was for the foreign widows and orphans (gentiles) that lived in Israel.[90] Therefore, ancient Jews "tithed" 23.33% a year! With this, I want to prove to you that what we consider the 'tithe,' does not have a literal parallel to the Old Testament after Christ's coming, but that it does have a parallel with its principles - honouring God as rightful Owner of everything we have, and that 10% should be our starting point and not our goal.

WHERE YOU PUT YOUR MONEY IS IMPORTANT

Although we have been talking about tithes and offerings mostly for the church or parish, the reality is that it is only a small part of giving.

I would like to give a caution here with regard to the people and organizations that we will help with our time, talent and treasures. These words are valid for both faith communities and secular organizations.

As early as the first century after Christ, there was a concern among the leaders of the Christian church for the appearance of those who, posing themselves as 'apostles,' 'preachers,' or 'prophets,' sought material gain through the preaching of the gospel. We can clearly see this concern in the Didache or "The Doctrine of the Twelve Apostles" (a document of the early church that came to light in 1875 in the city of Istanbul, Turkey).

---

88 See the fourth book of Moses, Numbers, chapter 18, verses 21 to 32.
89 See the fifth book of Moses, Deuteronomy, chapter 14, verses 22 to 29.
90 Same as previous one

The Didache states, for example, that any apostle or prophet who wanted more than bread for the road, or asks for money or demanded to be hosted for more than two days, should be considered false.[91]

In the 21st century, we can be more indulgent… but not a lot. Here are some guidelines to consider prior to giving to any organization or person:

- How many years does this organization or church have?
- Do they have concrete and clear goals, or are they trying to be everything for everybody?
  (The saying goes, Jack of all trades, Master of none")
- What is the reputation of its leader?
- How are Biblical principles and values reflected?
- Does the organization or church have regular financial reports?
- Are these reports available for the donors?
- Does the organization have an external auditor?
- Does the organization have a board of directors or is it a dictatorship?
- Are the board members related? If so, how many?
- What are the concrete results of the work of this organization?
- What percentage of the donations is used to ask for more donations?
- How is the salary of the leaders of the organization or church established?
- How many times the minimum wage does the leader earn?

I will leave the subject of generosity, as a key ingredient to financial success, with a story:

A beggar was asking for money at the side of the road when the famous Alexander the Great passed by. Alexander looked at him and, with a kindly gesture, gave him a few

---

91   Didache, chapter 11, verses 4 to 6, 9, 12. Taked from Justo L. González. Faith & Wealth. (New York: Harper-Collins, 1990), page 93.

gold coins. One of the servants of the great conqueror, surprised by the generosity of Alexander said, "My lord, some copper coins might have adequately satisfied the need of this beggar. Why give him gold?" The conqueror looked at his servant and wisely answered, "Some copper coins might have satisfied the need of the beggar; but the gold coins satisfy Alexander's generosity!"

Let's learn to give on a financial level that not only satisfies the physical needs of others, but above all, satisfies the generosity and integrity of our heart.

QUESTIONS AND PRACTICE FOR CHAPTER 9

1. What would be your biggest longing now that you know how to be prosperous?

2. What are your motivations for giving?

3. Do you remember the last time that you gave sacrificially? What were you able to learn from that experience?

4. Write down the principles you consider most important when talking about the attitude of a Christian who gives

5. How can you teach these lessons to your children?

NOTE:

Remember that you should continue with the task in item 3 that you began in chapter 4 (Biblical declarations to think about for 40 days).

See page 99

Chapter Ten

HAS GIVEN HERSELF TO GOD

DR. ANDRÉS PANASIUK

"Charm is deceptive, and beauty disappears,
but a woman who honours the Lord should be praised."
Proverbs 31:30

Some years ago, a book came into my hands that caused a profound impact not only on my life, but on my wife's as well. It is called "Surrender", a book that Nancy Leigh DeMoss published in 2006. The author develops the concept of surrendering. It shocked us so much that I've been preaching the subject all over the world since then. I would like to share with you a series of ideas that I have taken from this book, mixed with what it produced in me. This surrendering also includes the concept of submission, of self- denial.

This self-denial, which implies dying to self and surrendering completely to the will of God, is at the centre of God's plan of salvation for our life. [92] Around this attitude revolves everything we have written in this book and is the cornerstone in the process of enjoying Whole-life prosperity.

Nancy Leigh begins telling the story of Hiroo Onoda, a Japanese soldier on the island of Lubang, in the Philippines, who was isolated from his platoon and the rest of the world during World War 2. Despite the countless efforts to inform him that the war was over, Onoda continued the fight for 29 years until finally, on March 10, 1974 he surrendered his rusty sword to the Philippine authorities, thus becoming the last Japanese soldier to surrender.[93]

Surrendering is not easy. For those who have invited Jesus into our lives, the war is over, however surrendering is so hard.

The problem of renouncing and surrendering

The attitude of surrendering is at the heart of the conflict of the ages, at the centre of the problems that we have to face in our universe.

For example, during the first divine act that the Scriptures record, God carries out a control exercise over the laws of nature. He says, "Let there be light!" and the whole universe surrenders to His will to please Him and light appears in our history.[94]

When nature obeys God it is happy, 'satisfied.' The psalmist says, "You send rain on the mountains from your heavenly home, and

---

92   See Matthew 16:24, "If any of you want to come with me, you must forget yourself, carry your cross, and follow me". Same as, Mark 8:34 and Luke 14:27. GNT translation.

93   DeMoss, Nancy Leigh. Surrender. 2006

94   Same as previous note

you fill the earth with the fruit of your labour."[95] However, the problem of the ages began when Lucifer, an angel specially gifted by God, decided not to surrender his will to the King of Lights.

In the book of the prophet Isaiah we are told:

> *How you are fallen from heaven,*
> *O shining star, son of the morning!*
> *You have been thrown down to the earth,*
> *you who destroyed the nations of the world.*
> *For you said to yourself,*
> *'I will ascend to heaven and set my throne above God's stars.*
> *I will preside on the mountain of the gods*
> *far away in the north.*
> *I will climb to the highest heavens*
> *and be like the Most High.'*
> *Instead, you will be brought down to the place of the dead,*
> *down to its lowest depths.*[96]

Oswald Chambers, in his book "My Utmost for His Highest"[97], notes that "The concept of 'surrender' [resignation] does not mean surrendering our external life, but our will. When that is done, there is nothing else to do. There are very few crises in life. The great crisis is the renouncing of your own will".

In the last 50 years, people from first-world countries have made an important cultural change; they have abandoned the feeling of complete surrendering for the concept of "compromise,"[98] and the Body of Christ has been infected with that bug.

---

95   Psalm 104:13
96   Isaiah 14:12-15.
97   Chambers, Oswald. My Utmost for His Highest, 1927.
         Ver: http://www.oswaldchambers.co.uk
98   DeMoss, Nancy Leigh. Surrender. 2006

It is not rare today to listen to ministers invite people to make a 'commitment' to the Lord, instead of surrendering their lives to Christ.

A 'commitment' is something I do for you, I promise to do one thing for something else. Surrendering implies that I give myself to you. I surrender. You assume total control over me and do whatever you want of me.

Surrender is very different from commitment. But in the 21st century, people don't want to surrender. They would rather live the Christian life and still retain control. The Woman Who Prospers is a woman who gives herself completely into the hands of the Master; who completely surrenders to His will. She renounces herself and seeks to please her Lord.

The supreme example of surrender

The most important example we have of personal resignation and complete surrendering is found in the letter that Paul sent to his beloved friends in Philippians. He talks about the surrendering process that Jesus himself went through. [99]

In the eternal past, the Second Person of the Trinity, renounced Himself and surrendered to the will of the First. He surrendered presence, power, position, prestige... He gave up all to come live among us, to serve us and even die for us.

Some people incorrectly say that the Jews were guilty of the death of Jesus. Others say that the Romans were the guilty ones. Nobody was guilty of the death of Jesus. He gave His life of His own free

---

99   Philippians, 2:5-11

will.[100] It was an act of renouncement and surrendering to the will of His Father.

John opened for us an incredible window to what happened at Calvary. The Apostle says, "When Jesus had tasted it, he said, "It is finished!" Then he bowed his head and gave up his spirit."[101] (NLT)

Nobody killed Lord Jesus. He gave His live at His own will. What do you need to surrender to God?

It is interesting to note that, based on this complete act of rendition by the Lord Jesus, God the Father recognizes Him by giving everything back to His Son.

To the Philippians, the apostle Paul says, For this reason God raised him to the highest place above and gave him the name that is greater than any other name. And so, in honour of the name of Jesus all beings in heaven, on earth, and in the world below will fall on their knees, and all will openly proclaim that Jesus Christ is Lord, to the glory of God the Father."[102] Jesus' disciple John says in his Revelation, The world has now become the Kingdom of our Lord and of his Christ, and He will reign forever and ever."[103]

But… wait! This is not the end of the story. The true ending, the end of the story of humankind, the world and the entire universe, comes in a completely unexpected act on behalf of the Son of God. Paul says, Then the end will come; Christ will overcome all spiritual rulers, authorities, and powers, and will hand over the Kingdom to God the Father.   For Christ must rule until God defeats all enemies and puts them under his feet. [...]But when all things have been placed under Christ's rule, then he himself, the Son, will place

---

100 See Isaiah 53:10 and John 10:15.
101 John 19:30
102 Philippians 2:9-11
103 Revelation 11:5

himself under God, who placed all things under him; and God will rule completely over all."[104]

When the Son of God receives as a prize all the kingdoms of the world, all authority in the universe, when all things are submissive under His feet, (even Lucifer with all the rebel angels), He takes all these things in His hands, turns around, walks toward the Father's throne and, there once again, surrenders everything – even Himself – and places all at the feet of His Heavenly Father, in order to restore all things in the universe under the will of God.

What do you need to surrender to God?

The woman who really experiences God's prosperity in her life, is not the one who is the most beautiful, the richest or the most intelligent. It is the one that in an act of complete rendition, has surrendered herself in the arms of the Master.

What do you still want to control?
* Personal possessions?
* Money?
* Your marriage?
* Your children?
* Your home?
* Your business?
* Your dreams?
* Temptations?
* Sin in your life?

Today is the day to imitate the Son of God, take your life and surrender it completely and absolutely to the will and direction of God.

---

104 1 Corinthians 15:24-25, 28

There is an old hymn that clearly paints the kind of attitude that we need to close this subject and I would like to share it with you. Here are the lyrics for you to read and to sing if you know the melody!

All to Jesus I surrender,
All to Him I freely give;
I will ever love and trust Him,
In His presence daily live.

I surrender all,
I surrender all;
All to Thee, my blessed Saviour,
I surrender all.
All to Jesus I surrender,
Humbly at His feet I bow;
Worldly pleasures all forsaken,
Take me, Jesus, take me now.

All to Jesus I surrender,
Make me, Saviour, wholly Thine;
Let me feel the Holy Spirit,
Truly know that Thou art mine.

All to Jesus I surrender,
Lord, I give myself to Thee;
Fill me with Thy love and power,
Let Thy blessing fall on me.

All to Jesus I surrender,
Now I feel the sacred flame;
Oh, the joy of full salvation!
Glory, glory, to His Name!

Paraphrasing the preacher Henry Varley …

> The world is still to see
> What God is about to do
> With a woman completely
> Surrendered to Him
>
> You can be that woman!

QUESTIONS AND PRACTICE FOR CHAPTER 10

Think about it…

1. Have you experienced that resignation to yourself and surrendered to God? How and when was it?

2. If you still have not done it, think about this in prayer to the Lord. What is stopping you from doing it today?

3. Make a list of everything that you need to surrender to God …

NOTE:

Remember that you should continue with the task in item 3 that you began in chapter 4 (Biblical declarations to think about for 40 days).

See page 99

ABOUT COMPASS

Compass - finances God's way is a global, non-denominational movement teaching financial discipleship and generosity. The purpose is to serve churches, businesses, ministries, schools and other organisations by providing biblically-based solutions on handling money and possessions. Our vision is to see everyone, everywhere faithfully living by God's financial principles in all areas of their lives.

Global mission

Compass' mission is to help people everywhere to learn, apply and teach Gods financial and business principles. We are looking for three major outcomes.

To know Christ more intimately as we trust and obey Him, experiencing Christ at work.

To become free from worry, fear, stress and anxiety and then be free to serve and love the Lord and our neighbours.

To contribute to fulfilling the Great Commission by giving our money and other resources to fund the work of the Church.

The Compass Global Team is comprised of local leadership on 6 continents – Europe, Asia, South America, North America, Africa and the Indian sub-continent. Our continental offices serve more than 90 nations around the world.

To get in touch, please visit the Compass Global landing page www.compass1.global

Resources

Compass has developed a wide range of resources in a wide variety of formats, such as DVD based teaching, workshops, small group studies, e-books and online learning.

There are teaching resources for all ages, from small children through students to adults; with application to areas of life such as business, church, marriage and family.

Compass is active in over 80 nations over the globe and has resources in many languages. Contact our continental offices at www.compass1.global

To see specific English language resources, please visit the following online stores
US: www.compass1.org
UK: www.yourmoneycounts.org.uk
EU: www.compass1.eu

The Woman Who Prospers

SMALL GROUP STUDY

Get together with other women and join a small group to discuss *"The Woman Who Prospers."*

A small discussion group offers a place to connect with other believers in fellowship; to grow in your understanding of the Bible, as Jesus' own small group of disciples did; to meet the needs of others in your group in ministry; to become equipped for service; and to worship God through practicing godly behavior.

Small Group Bible study also offers a safe place to get your questions answered. If a small group setting is new to you, you'll be surprised how quickly you'll be helping others find answers as well.

When you are involved in a small group of other believers with varying backgrounds, chances are at least one other person in that group will be able to answer your specific questions. Certainly, as a group, you can determine to research and find answers to questions that cannot be answered in your regular meeting times. And aren't two or three or more heads better than one?

In your small group, you can also share your needs. At first, you may not feel comfortable sharing intimate details of your life, and you don't need to. But small group members exist to care for one another and to join in lifting one another's burdens before the Lord. Even if all you are willing to share is, "pray for me," then at least you can go out with the confidence that someone else is in fact praying for you. And God is listening.

Sometimes we face difficult circumstances. We enter hard places. We feel like no one understands. We have an enemy who loves to separate us from other believers. He attempts to affirm those thoughts that say, "No one wants me around." He wants us to feel alone.

But when women get together centered on God's Word, friendships form. We meet other women who've been there, who understand. God orchestrates relationships and brings us the right person to pray with us. We find instant prayer partners.

Contact your local Compass office for more details.
www.compass1.global